THE NEW MERMAIDS

A Chaste Maid in Cheapside

THE NEW MERMAIDS

General Editor

BRIAN GIBBONS
Professor of English Literature, University of Zürich

Previous general editors of the series have been:
PHILIP BROCKBANK
BRIAN MORRIS
ROMA GILL

A Chaste Maid in Cheapside

THOMAS MIDDLETON

Edited by ALAN BRISSENDEN

LONDON/A & C BLACK

NEW YORK/W W NORTON

Third impression 1988
Published by A & C Black (Publishers) Limited
35 Bedford Row, London WC1R 4JH

First published in this form 1968 by Ernest Benn Limited

© *Ernest Benn Limited 1968*

Published in the United States of America by
W W Norton & Company, Inc.
500 Fifth Avenue, New York, 10110

Printed in Great Britain by
Whitstable Litho Ltd., Whitstable, Kent

British Library Cataloguing in Publication Data

Middleton, Thomas, 1570?-1627?
  A chaste maid in Cheapside. – (The new mermaids).
  I. Title II. Brissenden, Alan III. Series
822'.3.

ISBN 0–7136–3084–1
ISBN 0–393–90023–1 (U.S.A.)

LIBBY'S

CONTENTS

ACKNOWLEDGEMENTS

A. H. BULLEN'S *The Works of Thomas Middleton* (8 vols. 1885–86) is still the standard edition but I have also used those of Dyce (5 vols. 1840) and Ellis (Mermaid Series, 2 vols. 1887–90) as well as R. J. Wall's unpublished dissertation, 'A Critical Edition of Thomas Middleton's *A Chast Mayd in Cheape-side*' (University of Michigan, 1958). *Shakespeare's Bawdy* (1956) by Eric Partridge, *A Topographical Dictionary to the Works of Shakespeare and his Fellow Dramatists* (Manchester, 1925) by E. H. Sugden and M. P. Tilley's *Dictionary of the Proverbs in England in the Sixteenth and Seventeenth Centuries* (Ann Arbor, 1950) have been indispensable reference books.

My sincere thanks are due to Mrs Edith Lack and Mrs Jane Delin, who saved me much tedium in hunting references, to my colleagues at the University of Adelaide, especially F. H. Mares, M. Bryn Davies and G. W. Turner, and to A. M. Gibbs of the University of Leeds. I am also grateful to Miss Pat Story for her typing, Miss Rebecca Foale for her cartography and the General Editors for their patience. To my wife and family I owe a special debt for accepting so nobly and for so long the presence of another woman in the house.

Note to new impression

I have taken the opportunity to correct misprints and make alterations and additions, some of them the result of having directed a production of the play in 1971.

Since 1968, when this edition of *A Chaste Maid in Cheapside* was first published, two others have appeared. The first, edited by Charles Barber for the Fountainwell series (Edinburgh, 1969), has a brief introduction interesting particularly for its Note on the Text. The second, edited by R. B. Parker for the Revels series (1969), contains full and informative notes, a stimulating introduction which pays special attention to staging, and several appendices, including a discussion of William Gaskill's 1966 production for London's Royal Court Theatre.

I am happy to acknowledge the kindness of Miss Elizabeth Sweeting, Administrator of the Oxford Playhouse, who sent me details of the O.U.D.S. production of the play in 1970.

A.B.

ABBREVIATIONS

Q	The edition of 1630.
Bullen	A. H. Bullen, *The Works of Thomas Middleton* (1885–86).
Dyce	Alexander Dyce, *The Works of Thomas Middleton* (1840).
ed.	editions other than this.
sl.	slang.
s.d.	stage direction.
s.p.	speech prefix.
C.H.E.L.	*Cambridge History of English Literature*
MLQ	*Modern Language Quarterly*
MLR	*Modern Language Review*
N&Q	*Notes and Queries*
N.S.	New Series
O.E.D.	*Oxford English Dictionary*
PMLA	*Publications of the Modern Language Association of America*
PQ	*Philological Quarterly*
RES	*Review of English Studies*
SEL	*Studies in English Literature*
SP	*Studies in Philology*
Stud.Bibl.	*Studies in Bibliography*
Survey	John Stow, *A Survey of London*, ed. C. L. Kingsford (Oxford, 1908).
Wall	R. J. Wall, 'A Critical Edition of Thomas Middleton's *A Chast Mayd in Cheape-side*', unpubl. diss. (Michigan, 1958).

INTRODUCTION

THE AUTHOR

THOMAS MIDDLETON'S life spans the greatest period in English drama. He was born in 1580, being christened at St Lawrence Jewry on 18 April, and was buried on 4 July 1627 at St Mary's, Newington Butts, about a mile south of Southwark.[1] His father, William, was a bricklayer and gentleman with his own coat of arms, who owned property near the Curtain Theatre in Shoreditch and at Limehouse he died in January 1585/86 and his widow, Anne, married an impoverished but ambitious adventurer, Thomas Harvey, whose principal aim seems to have been to get his hands on the Middleton property. This also appears to have been the reason for Allen Waterer's marriage to Avice Middleton, Thomas's sister, in 1596. Until 1603, by which time both Anne and Waterer were dead, legal squabbles over the properties disrupted the family; even after her first husband's death, Avice and her second husband, John Empson, took up litigation, still over the property, against Waterer's brother. Middleton himself probably married about 1602, as his son Edward was aged nineteen in 1623. His wife Mary was the granddaughter of the composer and organist John Marbeck and her brother was for a time an actor with the Admiral's Men. She was probably the Maulyn Marbeck who was christened on 9 July 1575 at St Dunstan's in the West; this agrees with the name of the playwright's widow, given as Magdalen, who applied in February 1627/28 for a gift of money from the city of London; she was granted twenty nobles, but was probably little more trouble to the aldermen as she died in the following July and was buried at Newington.

The playwright matriculated at Queen's College, Oxford, the most popular college of the time, in April 1598 and although in 1600 he sold his share of the family property to his brother-in-law Waterer so that he could stay there he had to return to London to help his mother in one of her lawsuits in 1601 and apparently did not graduate. He was then said to have been seen in London 'daily accompanying the players'.[2] By the time he was twenty he had published some verse, *The Wisdom of Solomon Paraphrased* (1597), a

[1] See R. H. Barker, *Thomas Middleton* (New York, 1958), pp. 1–25 for a summary of findings on Middleton's life.
[2] See P. G. Phialas, 'Middleton's Early Contact with the Law', *SP*, LII (1955), 186–194.

tedious and lengthy piece best forgotten, *Micro-Cynicon* (1599), an attempt at Marstonian satire, and *The Ghost of Lucrece* (1600), a dull poem in the complaint tradition. In 1602 Henslowe notes him collaborating with Munday, Drayton, Webster and perhaps others on a lost play, *Caesar's Fall*, and two years later he published two prose tracts attacking low life vices. By this time he had almost certainly begun his career as a playwright with *The Family of Love* (*c*. 1602), a lively satire on sectaries in which he uses the twin themes of sex and wealth for the first time. The fact that his sister Avice's brother-in-law was a Brownist who had been in Newgate for his beliefs may have significance for Middleton's consistent ridicule of Puritans, but they were fair game for many other writers of the time.

Of about forty dramatic works that have been ascribed to Middleton at some time, thirteen plays have been suggested as his unaided work,[3] the rest being collaborations or masks and entertainments. He wrote and produced a number of pageants for the city of London from 1613 on and in 1620 was appointed City Chronologer to record the memorable acts and occurrences of the city, a post in which he was succeeded by Ben Jonson.

Middleton's published plays fall conveniently, if loosely, into three groups, city comedies, which end triumphantly with *A Chaste Maid in Cheapside* (1611–13), romances like *The Widow* (1616) and the great tragedies, *The Changeling*, with Rowley (1622), and *Women Beware Women* (1621–27); in 1624 he wrote the brilliant occasional satire *A Game at Chess*, which ran for nine days at the Globe and got the King's Men into trouble with their patron.[4] Middleton, as well as the players, was summoned before the Privy Council, but no action seems to have been taken when he failed to appear, and his son Edward was called to answer for him.

His early unaided plays were written for the children's companies of Paul's and Blackfriars; after they disbanded in 1606 he wrote for Prince Henry's (formerly the Admiral's) Men and the Lady Elizabeth's company, but mostly for the King's Men. It is clear that his early life greatly influenced his writing: his father's house was in Ironmonger's Lane, off Cheapside, and he was in every sense a Londoner; at the same time he remembered Oxford with affection and his university fools are all from Cambridge; sex and property hunger were closely related in the unfortunate course of his family's life after his father's death, and the bitterness and dismay which he

---

[3] See C. Hoy, 'The Shares of Fletcher and his Collaborators in the Beaumont and Fletcher Canon', V, *Stud. Bibl.*, XIII (1960), 77–106.

[4] For a discussion of Middleton's relationship with King James see W. Power, 'Thomas Middleton *vs.* King James I', *N & Q*, CCII (1957), 526–534.

probably felt at that time may have resulted in the attitudes which colour the greater part of his best work.

DATE AND SOURCES

The Lady Elizabeth's company was not formed until 1611 and most probably left the Bankside by the end of 1613, so that these approximate limits can be given for the composition of *A Chaste Maid*. Fleay stated that the play was *The Proud Maid's Tragedy* acted at court on 25 February 1612 and Chambers unaccountably finds nothing improbable with the suggestion.[5] The only real connection apparent between the two plays, however, is the company which acted them both.

Internal evidence suggested by R. C. Bald and R. J. Wall[6] indicates 1613 rather than earlier. Bald draws attention to the tightening of laws against killing and eating meat during Lent in 1613, which gives a topical background for the scene with the promoters (II, ii); the reinforcement of these Lenten acts, however, was begun in 1608, and repeated each year, so this evidence is not unassailable. Wall sees the flattering portrayal of the watermen in Act IV as being support for their agitation against the building of theatres north of the Thames; a petition was sent to King James in January 1614, as a falling off of the theatrical trade to the Bankside during 1613 had meant a considerable loss to them. It may be added that the main relevant passage (IV, ii, 6–12) specifically puts the Blackfriars theatre in a bad light, presenting it as a rowdy and dangerous place. (No evidence has yet been found that the incident described really occurred.)

Another indication of 1613 as the most likely date may lie in Allwit's boast that when his wife is in childbed

> A lady lies not in like her; there's her embossings,
> Embroiderings, spanglings, and I know not what,
>
> (I, ii, 32–33)

and the christening guest's comment, 'See gossip and she lies not in like a countess' (III, ii, 101). These remarks would have had particular relevance soon after the extravagant lying in of the Countess of Salisbury at the end of January 1613 (see note to III, ii, 101). There may also be significance in Allwit's calling the baby 'little countess' (II, ii, 27).

[5] E. K. Chambers, *The Elizabethan Stage* (Oxford, 1923), III, 441.
[6] R. C. Bald, 'The Chronology of Middleton's Plays', *MLR*, XXXII (1937), 40; R. J. Wall, pp. 5–10.

Although none of the evidence is conclusive, the most probable time of the play's first performance would seem to be soon after Lent in 1613.

Middleton appears to have invented the stories of the play, though he may have taken ideas from several sources. Elizabeth Buckingham[7] argues persuasively that an epigram in Campion's *Art of English Poesie* (1602) is a direct source for the Allwit-Whorehound plot (see Appendix A); a situation similar to Allwit's is also the subject of a contemporary ballad, 'Who would not be a cuckold', which makes special reference to social climbing in the city (see Appendix A). A. H. Gilbert[8] suggests that Middleton may have used an Italian treatise on marriage; and Dekker's *Bachelor's Banquet* (1603) could have provided him with material for the christening scene. It is just possible that he may have intended personal satire in the character of Yellowhammer, since a suit for debt was brought against Middleton, among others, by Robert Keysar, a goldsmith of Cheapside, in 1609.

THE PLAY

First mentioned in 1067 as 'Westceape'[9] and as 'Chepsyde' in 1510, the wide street of Cheapside was the old market place of London, extending from the north-east corner of St Paul's churchyard to the Poultry. Down the centre stood four structures; at the western end the Little, or Pissing Conduit, then one of the twelve crosses set up by Edward I to mark the resting-places of Queen Elinor's body on its way from Lincoln to Westminster Abbey, next was the Standard, a square pillar with a conduit, and a statue of Fame on the top, and at the eastern end the Great Conduit, first built in 1285, to which water was piped from Paddington. The conduits ran wine on special occasions and served as stages for shows, Cheapside being on the main processional route through the city between the fourteenth and seventeenth centuries. Many of the side streets were named after trades, and the Mermaid tavern probably stood in Bread Street. Goldsmiths' Row, the part of Cheapside between Bread and Friday streets, was to John Stow 'the most beautiful frame of fair houses and shops that be within the walls of London, or elsewhere in England . . . It containeth in number ten fair dwelling-houses and fourteen

[7] E. L. Buckingham, 'Campion's *Art of English Poesie* and Middleton's *Chaste Maid in Cheapside*', *PMLA*, XLIII (1928), 784–791.
[8] A. H. Gilbert, 'The Prosperous Wittol in Giovanni Battista Modio and Thomas Middleton', *SP*, XLI (1944), 235–237.
[9] Anglo-Saxon 'ceap' = 'barter'.

shops, all in one frame, uniformly built four storeys high.'[10] Cheapside itself, he said, 'is worthily called, the Beauty of London'.[11]

This, then, is the setting for Middleton's culminating achievement in comedy, *A Chaste Maid in Cheapside*. The comedies he wrote for the children's companies, especially *Michaelmas Term*, *A Mad World, My Masters* and *A Trick to Catch the Old One* (all *c.* 1604–1607), show a mastery of material and a firm satiric intent, but none attains the marvellous unity of tone and headlong vitality of *A Chaste Maid*. Although the play was largely neglected by critics until the 1930's—Eliot, for instance, does not mention it in his essay on Middleton—Swinburne acclaimed it as having much 'humour, though very little chastity' and engagingly described it as 'a play of quite exceptional freedom and audacity, and certainly one of the drollest and liveliest that ever broke the bounds of propriety or shook the sides of merriment'. This success may have been due to its being written for an adult company and a public stage,[12] or it may have been a process of maturing in the playwright. For whatever reason, he welds into a complex whole the themes of corruption, money and sex which are particularly his so that we laugh, often uproariously, even while we are chilled with faint horror and sickened with disgust. In its attitudes to vice and punishment *A Chaste Maid* looks forward to the later plays, especially *Women Beware Women*, in many ways its equivalent in tragedy.

All the main characters are corrupt to some degree, even the lovers, Moll Yellowhammer and Touchwood Junior, having to deceive so that they can marry. The tentacles of corruption stretch back into the past and forward into the future: Moll's mother was 'lightsome, and quick' two years before she was married (I, i, 8); her father has kept a whore 'and had a bastard,/By Mistress Anne' (IV, i, 272–73) while Lady Kix, charged with barrenness, indignantly cries, 'I barren!/ 'Twas otherways with me when I was at court' (III, iii, 55–56). Even a minor figure like the Country Wench is doubly corrupt—she claims at first that she was a virgin before meeting Touchwood Senior (II, i, 70) but later says that her present child is her fifth (II, i, 104), and Lady Kix speaks of her sister who has had twins, seven months after marriage (II, i, 171). The action of the play moves in an ambience of illicit sex, which will continue in the future as Touchwood Senior becomes a professional

[10] *Survey*, I, 345.
[11] John Stow, *Annals of Great Britain* (1615), p. 859.
[12] See T. S. Eliot, 'Thomas Middleton' (1927), *Selected Essays* (1951), pp. 161–170; A. C. Swinburne, 'Thomas Middleton', *Thomas Middleton*, ed. H. Ellis, I (1887), xviii–xix; M. C. Bradbrook, *The Growth and Structure of Elizabethan Comedy* (1955), p. 161.

adulterer (V, iv, 83) and the Allwits decide to set up a brothel in the Strand (V, i, 170).

Most of the sexual relationships in the play are directed by greed for riches, and this greed overrides all else, especially affecting family loyalties.[13] Allwit, the complacent cuckold, and his wife live off Sir Walter Whorehound, Mistress Allwit's lover and father of her seven children; Davy, Sir Walter's kinsman, hopes the wealthy knight will die so that he can gain an inheritance. The Allwits are a commercial enterprise rather than a married couple bound by mutual love; they have little or no feeling, either for each other or anyone else. There is perhaps more human feeling between Maudlin Yellowhammer and her husband, but they have little for their children except in so far as they are business assets—Tim, the Cambridge boy, because he is rising socially in the world and going to marry a Welsh heiress, Moll because she is the bait to land a rich knight, even though he may be diseased. In each case the marriage will bring to the tradesman that socially necessary commodity, land. Their attitudes are shaped almost exclusively by their lust for money. When Moll appears to be dying, Maudlin tries to revive her by saying, 'Look but once up, thou shalt have all the wishes of thy heart/That wealth can purchase' (V, ii, 95–96), and when she is thought dead, their hopes of riches return with the thought that Tim is going to marry—'We'll not lose all at once, somewhat we'll catch' (V, ii, 116).

Her cruelty to Moll is due also to the frustration of Maudlin's social ambitions, for the Yellowhammers are more socially conscious than any of the other characters. The goldsmith stresses that Moll, being his daughter, is 'no gentlewoman' (I, i, 189), and that when Tim proceeds to his degree he will be 'Sir Yellowhammer then/ Over all Cambridge, and that's half a knight' (I, i, 155–156).

Wealth and sex are the means of uniting bonds rather than destroying them in the other two families in the play. Touchwood Senior and his wife, who have had to part because they have too many children and can afford no more, are invited to live at the expense of Sir Oliver Kix, whose own marriage is retrieved when Touchwood Senior impregnates Lady Kix, Sir Oliver believing, of course, that he himself is the prospective father. These two families are treated with less seriousness, less bitterness than the Allwits and Yellowhammers. No shudder lies behind the laughter aroused by the Touchwoods and Kixes. This is partly because Kix is a cheerful old fool, and there is genuine affection between him and his wife,

[13] This aspect of the play is discussed in an important article by Samuel Schoenbaum, 'A Chaste Maid in Cheapside and Middleton's City Comedy', in Studies in the English Renaissance Drama, ed. Josephine W. Bennett et. al. (New York, 1959), pp. 287–309.

and love between the Touchwoods; there is none between the Allwits and little between the Yellowhammers.

In an elaborate analysis of the plots in *A Chaste Maid*, Richard Levin[14] argues that the families balance each other and that the two married couples and their attendant cuckolds are in symmetrical opposition. There are, however, other contrasts which Levin's scheme, brilliant as it is, does not have room to include. The Yellowhammers and the Kixes are opposed, for instance, in the way the first want to be rid of their children and the second want to get children; they are linked in their common reason—greed for land and money. A Kix child will disinherit Sir Walter, and the marriages of Moll and Tim will enrich their parents, or so they believe. Ruby Chatterji[15] takes issue with Levin on the grounds that he over-emphasizes plot relationships, and she argues that the family is the functional unit which becomes the focus of the play.

Miss Chatterji also discusses the punishment of the characters, suggesting that Sir Walter alone is punished because 'he undermines the very concept of marriage in a citizen household, and also seeks to thrive on the barrenness of another couple'.[16] The fertile Touch-wood Senior does this, however, and he is rewarded. The important point is that Sir Walter is punished physically: the scales fall from his eyes and he sees the ordinary world; he can no longer stay in the callous, inhuman world of the Allwits and Yellowhammers, and fundamentally he is better off; but the necessary price for salvation is physical mortification. The other characters are punished too, but their punishment lies in their spiritual desiccation. Hippolito, in *Women Beware Women*, speaks of man coming by destruction, 'which oft-times/He wears in his own bosom' (II, i, 3–4),[17] and this is true of most of the characters in *A Chaste Maid*. Sir Walter at least has a spiritual victory of sorts.

The knight has his revelation, the others do not, and the theme of blindness, developed so fully in the great tragedies, is quietly present in *A Chaste Maid*. For Sir Walter, his misbegotten children stand between him and the 'sight of Heaven' (V, i, 72), for instance. The main use of the theme, however, is characteristically ironic—the Welsh Gentlewoman's mountains are so high 'you cannot see the top of 'em' (I, i, 137); the motto inside Touchwood Junior's ring for

---

[14] R. Levin, 'The Four Plots of *A Chaste Maid in Cheapside*', *RES*, N.S., XVI (1965), 14–24.

[15] R. Chatterji, 'Theme, Imagery and Unity in *A Chaste Maid in Cheapside*', *Renaissance Drama*, VIII (1965), 105–126.

[16] Chatterji, p. 115.

[17] Unless otherwise stated, references to Middleton's works apart from *A Chaste Maid* are to the eight volume edition by A. H. Bullen (1885–86).

Moll is, 'Love that's wise, blinds parents' eyes' (I, i, 200); Yellowhammer wears glasses, but is so blind to what is going on that he is
wryly advised to 'put on a pair more' (III, i, 33), and the foolish
Tim, bewailing his marriage to a whore, says, 'I was promised
mountains,/But there's such a mist, I can see none of 'em' (V, iv,
99–100).

Irony informs the whole structure of *A Chaste Maid* and con-
tributes to its remarkable unity.[18] The relationship of the Allwits and
the Kixes provides a good example of irony in the plot. Allwit, who
lives off the proceeds of his cuckoldom by Sir Walter Whorehound,
is set against Sir Oliver, who pays Touchwood Senior for making
him a cuckold. Sir Walter descends from riches to poverty, believes
he has taken a life and is turned from the house he maintains;
Touchwood rises to wealth by creating life and is invited to make his
home with the ignorant victim and his family. Sir Walter repents of
his sin, Touchwood looks forward to a prosperous sinful future. The
plots are linked, again ironically, by Touchwood Junior, who
deprives Sir Walter of his bride, Moll, and, by encouraging his
brother's adventure with the Kixes, disinherits him as well. The
audience can hardly draw a moral from Sir Walter's repentance, as it
is counterbalanced by Touchwood's cheerful acceptance of the
lucrative role of adulterer. Middleton, unlike John Marston, is
detached enough to let the points make themselves, one situation
the inversion of the other.

Always reinforcing the irony of plot and action is Middleton's use
of words. The title of the play itself is ironic at first glance, since
Cheapside maids were not, apparently, noted for their chastity.
Dekker writes that 'A fair wench is to be seen every morning in some
shop in Cheapside: And in summer afternoons the self-same fair
opens her booth at one of the garden-houses about Bunhill'.[19] The
language of the play often gains ironic force from the surrounding
action, as in the case of the posy for Moll's wedding ring (I, i, 200).
Sometimes irony is due to the character who is saying the words, for
example the Puritans in Act III, who can scarcely speak without
producing *double entendre*. Subtlety and depth can come in single

---

[18] As well as those already mentioned, writers who comment on this aspect of
the play include U. M. Ellis-Fermor, *The Jacobean Drama* (1961), pp.
135–138, and R. B. Parker, 'Middleton's Experiments with Comedy and
Judgement', in *Jacobean Theatre*, ed. J. R. Brown and B. Harris (1960), pp.
179–199.

[19] Thomas Dekker, *The Owl's Almanac* (1618), p. 8. For evidence that
whores frequented the vicinity of Bunhill see E. H. Sugden, *A Topographical
Dictionary to the Works of Shakespeare and his Fellow Dramatists* (Manchester, 1925), pp. 83–84.

phrases, as when Allwit says he shall be 'hare-mad' (III, ii, 216); hares grow wild in the breeding season, around March, the time of the play's action, but even though his wife is breeding, Allwit is not the cause. A single word can illuminate character and situation and condense several implications; 'green goose' (II, ii, 83), for instance, is both a young goose, ready for making into goose pie, but also a simpleton, and a cuckold; 'smelt' and 'gudgeons' (IV, ii, 51, 53) both imply foolishness and contribute to the aura of stupidity which surrounds Tim Yellowhammer.

The audience is soon made aware of the technique of *double entendre* which is essential to the play's language; Maudlin's reminiscences about her 'dancing master' (I, i, 14–17) are sexual, as are such phrases as Allwit's reference to the knight's supporting him and his wife 'with a prop' (III, ii, 76) and Sir Oliver Kix's firm assertion 'Nay I'm not given to standing' (III, iii, 137). There is a good deal of more obvious punning, especially in the slapstick scenes with Tim and the Welsh Gentlewoman, and Middleton has fun with broken Latin, in one case fashioning nearly a page of dialogue on one Latin phrase (IV, i, 59–80).

Wordplay is an essential part of the imagery which is also important for the play's unity.[20] Images of food and animals, for instance, emphasize the themes of greed and carnality. In using these images, Middleton may be compared with Jonson in *Volpone* and Webster in his two tragedies. The Duchess of Malfi asks her murderers to tell her brothers that they may 'feed in quiet' when she is dead; Mistress Allwit *enceinte* is 'as great as she can wallow' (I, ii, 6) and 'even upon the point of grunting' (I, ii, 31). The theme of double-dealing which occurs in all the plots is supported by gaming images; Touchwood Senior 'ne'er played/Yet under a bastard' (II, i, 55–56), Allwit is 'but one peep above a servingman' (I, ii, 68) and Sir Walter and Touchwood Junior talk in gambling terms as they duel. Connected with this gaming imagery are the many commercial images in the play, like Tim's remark that 'Gold into white money was never so changed' (V, ii, 20) as his half-drowned sister's complexion. It is noticeable that the image patterns of *Women Beware Women* are markedly similar to those of *A Chaste Maid*.

The imagery illuminates the corrupt world of Cheapside, and at the same time enlarges the application of Middleton's moral criticism beyond it. Animals feed off one another, foul one another's nests, and will, for the most part, go on doing so. His attack on vice ranges widely, from small follies like the Puritans' dislike of red hair, because it was Judas's colour, to the Puritans themselves; from belief

[20] See also Chatterji, *op. cit.*

in quack medicines, 'waters', to the grand heartlessness and cupidity of the Allwits and Yellowhammers of the world. Middleton's satire is harsh, and the play is not lighthearted, as Barker remarks.[21] But neither does he begin to lose control, as L. C. Knights suggests in an unbalanced but thought provoking essay.[22] He is, indeed, never more firmly in control of his material.

Like Swift in *A Modest Proposal*, Middleton reverses normal values so convincingly that the audience accepts the world of Cheapside as the real world. Topsy-turvydom reaches its satiric apogee in the Allwit-Whorehound relationship, where the cuckolder takes over from the husband so completely that he can jealously accuse the husband of daring to sleep with his own wife and the husband protest that he has not. The comic climax of the play is provided by the reversal of a funeral into a marriage. This world of inverted values and relationships had been arrived at by Chapman in *The Widow's Tears* (*c*. 1605), where a husband cuckolds himself to prove his wife's constancy (she claiming later that she knew who it was all the time), and a pronouncement is made that 'It shall be the only note of love to the husband to love the wife: and none shall be more kindly welcome to him than he that cuckolds him' (V, i, 306–308). It is exactly this position which Middleton uses to criticize society in *A Chaste Maid*. Where Chapman's play is a development of the action to that point, however, Middleton uses the situation as the continuing condition—Sir Walter's association with the Allwits may end, but Touchwood Senior takes on a similar vocation with the Kixes.

The attitude is serious, but the realization is comic. Sir Walter, even in repentance, is overdrawn so that there is a certain amount of undercutting; yet he probably gains the sympathy of most of the audience. Similarly, the moment of Moll's apparent death emphasizes by contrast the callousness of her parents. We may laugh at Maudlin's 'O, I could die with music' (V, ii, 50) as Moll sings her last strain, but the laughter has an undercurrent of disgust. Here Middleton is again using an ironic technique to make his point. (I am told that Moll's song created a moment of genuine pathos, making the comedy all the blacker, when the play was performed in London in 1966. Quite unexpected, this effect was, as the producer William Gaskill said, one of those things that 'just happen' in the theatre.)

The balance of the plots, the consistency of the themes and attitudes, irony, its attendant word usage and imagery all contribute to the play's unity. Two other related aspects of Middleton's

[21] Barker, *op. cit.*, p. 86.

[22] L. C. Knights, *Drama and Society in the Age of Jonson* (1962), p. 224.

technique are the pace of the action and the localization in time and place. There is no pause in the play's movement; even the two big soliloquies, those of Allwit (I, ii, 12–57) and Touchwood Senior (II, i, 43–63), extend the action into the past and the future. The scenes are arranged so that the action flows in counterpoint. At the end of Act I, for instance, the Allwit-Whorehound *ménage* makes ready for its seventh birth with all the family present for the occasion. Act II begins with the too fecund Touchwoods parting because they cannot afford more children. There are similar juxtapositions throughout the play, providing a tension which helps keep alive the interest of the audience.

By making the action take place in Lent, Middleton gives his play a particular focus, and heightens the satire on lust and sensuality. The religious significance of the time accentuates Cheapside's mockery of true spiritual values, which are travestied by the christening, where a whoremaster stands godfather to his own bastard, Puritans get drunk and a cuckold beamingly takes the credit for a child not his own. The Country Wench's ruse to get rid of her bastard recalls the play of Mak the shepherd in the Towneley Cycle, and the general air of gluttony and greed which pervades the play is heightened by the contrast given by the season.

Localization of place is a marked characteristic of the play. 'We are eavesdropping on Elizabethan London—the real thing, and not some Italianate mock-up' was the comment of a reviewer who saw a revival of the play in 1956.[23] Middleton was a true Londoner and the city becomes not merely a setting for his characters but a character itself in the action. The streets, the wharves, the taverns, the stairs are all real and necessary. This precision gives a definition and clarity to the action; it provides as well a firm framework to contain outrageously grotesque figures like Maudlin Yellowhammer and the monstrous Allwit. One of Middleton's richest achievements is to persuade his audience to accept the inflated perversity of his characters and their situations; his success is at least partly due to the strict accuracy of the scene. While irony may be the most powerful internal force binding the play together, the physical setting is the strongest external means of unity.

THE VERSE

The dialogue and the verse contribute much to the pace of the play. Colloquial abbreviations are constantly used ('is't' for 'is it',

[23] N.S., 'A Chaste Maid in Cheapside', *Manchester Guardian*, 29 November 1956.

'ha't' for 'have it', for instance) and there are several passages of
dialogue in short, chopped up lines which promote an air of urgency.
By the time Middleton wrote *A Chaste Maid in Cheapside* his verse
had become a highly refined instrument, sensitive to its context and
its content.[24] The smug complacency of Allwit, for instance, is
reflected rhythmically in his soliloquy, so that he sounds like a
grocer checking off the items on a big order.

> I walk out in a morning, come to breakfast,
> Find excellent cheer, a good fire in winter,
> Look in my coal house about midsummer eve,
> That's full, five or six chaldron, new laid up;
> Look in my back yard, I shall find a steeple
> Made up with Kentish faggots, which o'erlooks
> The waterhouse and the windmills; I say nothing
> But smile, and pin the door. When she lies in,
> As now she's even upon the point of grunting,
> A lady lies not in like her . . .   (I, ii, 23–32)

The change in rhythm in the last lines here points up a transition
from outdoors, where there are natural elements, wind and water
(and we may note the ironic compression of phallic and religious
elements in the word 'steeple'), to the unnaturalness indoors, where a
husband acts the pander and the wife, animal-like, is 'upon the point
of grunting'.

A broader, more discursive rhythm is used for a scene like the
separation of Touchwood and his wife (II, i, 1–42) and the balanced
metre allows for an occasionally epigrammatic tone, as in

> Some only can get riches and no children,
> We only can get children and no riches.
>   (II, i, 11–12)

The most striking use of Middleton's more flowing style is found in
the scene of Whorehound's repentance and rejection (V, i). He uses
rhyme sparingly, most often to conclude a scene, but also occasionally within a scene to heighten the emotion, as when Moll and
Touchwood Junior are about to be married (III, i).

As R. J. Wall points out, nineteenth-century editions of the play
give a misleading idea of the verse. 'The editors do not seem to have
been concerned with capturing the spirit of Middleton's *A Chast
Mayd*', he comments. 'Their editorial policy aimed, in effect, at

---

[24] Commenting on the maturity of the verse in another play, *Hengist, King of
Kent* (1616–1620), R. C. Bald has remarked that 'the change from the earlier
to the later style is first observable in *A Chaste Maid in Cheapside*, which
comes at the very end of his early comic period'. (Middleton, *Hengist, King of
Kent*, ed. R. C. Bald (New York, 1938), p. xv.)

"polishing" Middleton, at "perfecting" his style by regularizing his verse and smoothing his sentence structure.'[25] He discusses a number of examples of their practice including one in which the editors even rearranged lines set up as verse in the quarto, 'apparently for no other reason than to regularize the lines. . . . In [III, i, 28–30], the quarto gives the lines as follows:

> Was this the politike fetch, thou misticall baggage
> Thou disobedient strumpet,
> And were so wise to send for her to such an end.

Dyce and Bullen present the lines in the following manner, robbing the second line of its stress, and of the pause which should follow it:

> Was this the politic fetch, thou mystical baggage,
> Thou disobedient strumpet!—And were [you]
> So wise to send for her to such an end?'[26]

Wall points out that the action of the scene, which demands a pause after 'strumpet', explains the line division of the quarto.

Rearrangement of the lines, smoothing out of the metre and expanding contractions of speech change the impact of the verse on the reader and, since it is this impact which affects the way the actors will speak and interpret the lines, such alterations ultimately affect the characters and their situations. The irregular verse, which perturbed the earlier editors, in fact indicates Middleton's confidence and the flexibility of his medium.

[25] Wall, p. 33.
[26] Wall, p. 37.

NOTE ON THE TEXT

SIR HENRY HERBERT licensed the play for printing on 8 April 1630 and it was published in quarto in the same year. This is the only known early edition; fifteen copies are accessible and the present text has been prepared from a collation of photographic reproductions of those in the Library of Congress and the Henry E. Huntington, Folger and Harvard University libraries. (The Harvard copy is incomplete, lacking the K gathering and the lower part of sig. I4.) A Xerox print of the Huntington copy was used as the working text.

The few variants which occur in no way affect the meaning, but indicate that corrections were made as the play was going through the press. Pages 50, 51, 54 and 55 (sigs. H1^v, H2^r, H3^v and H4^r) are incorrectly numbered 36, 33, 40 and 37 in the Folger and Library of Congress copies, for example, while the Harvard and Huntington copies are paginated correctly, indicating that they were printed later in the run. The only bibliographical study of the play is R. J. Wall's, in his unpublished dissertation, and he concludes from an examination of seven copies that such variants as are to be found are textually unimportant.

The only editions after the quarto are those of Dyce (1840), Bullen (1885–86), which is virtually a reprint of Dyce's, and Havelock Ellis's (1887–90), in the earlier Mermaid series, which was based on a collation of those of Dyce and Bullen. Inconsistent in their modernization, cavalier in their treatment of the verse, and laborious in their punctuation, these nineteenth-century editions at least made this play, and many others, accessible to the student and the general reader.

The quarto seems to have been printed from a carefully prepared manuscript; it has few of the contractions and punctuation peculiar to Middleton's own hand[27] and except in one place it does not appear to be very close to the prompt book. The one instance is the long direction for the entry of the lovers' funeral (V, iv). The list of characters, the careful act divisions and the general tidiness of the text argue for the preparation of a scribal copy especially for the printing house.

Punctuation in the quarto relies heavily on the comma and on capitalization. There are relatively few full stops. The effect gained is one of lively conversational speech. While this kind of punctuation

[27] See Middleton, *A Game at Chesse*, ed. R. C. Bald (Cambridge, 1929), pp. 34, 171–173.

still works when the lines are spoken aloud, it becomes more difficult when read on the page; I have tried to preserve the original vitality by punctuating lightly, and while the quarto consistently uses a vocative capital (e.g., 'How is't with you Sir?'; V, i, 36), I have decapitalized but not inserted a vocative comma except where its absence would impair the sense. Also in the interests of pace I have retained the contractions and elisions which occur throughout the play. Names are normalized and speech prefixes expanded, oaths are regularized without an apostrophe ('Foot', not ''Foot') and all lines of verse begin with capitals.

The quarto has no scene divisions but gives Latin headings for the acts, from *Actus Primus* to *Actus Quintus*; these become Act I, Act II and so on. Editorial stage directions and other additions are enclosed in square brackets, *Ex[eunt]* indicating that the quarto has *Exit* used inappropriately.

STAGE HISTORY

A Chaste Maid is the only extant play certainly known to have been presented at the Swan Theatre, which, by happy chance, is the subject of the only contemporary drawing of an Elizabethan playhouse interior so far discovered.[28] (See p. xxxi and notes pp. 2, 95.) Apart from the statement on the title page that it 'hath beene often acted at the Swan on the Banke-side' there appear to be no contemporary allusions to the play, nor any record of its performance until this century, when Frederick May produced the play for a season beginning on 26 November 1956 for the Leeds University Union theatre group. This was a modern dress version, with jazz, rock and roll, blues songs and sweaters and jeans. It did not succeed for the critic of the *Manchester Guardian*, who concluded, 'All the same, it whets the appetite. Now let us see the "Chaste Maid" in her true colours'. *The Yorkshire Post* viewed it more kindly as 'unusual, imaginative and intriguing' and thought it better to have the young players 'succeed in their natural environment than . . . fail in the semblance of a Jacobean costume charade'.

In his introduction to the Revels edition of the play (1969), R. B. Parker lists five subsequent student productions at: (1) Leverett House, Harvard University, Christmas 1956, directed by Alfred Drake; (2) the Embassy Theatre, Swiss Cottage, directed by William Gaskill for the Central School of Speech and Drama, 10 March 1961; (3) University of Southampton, March 1962; (4) Jesus College, Cambridge University, directed by Martin Short, 14 and 15 June 1964; (5) St Michael's College, University of Toronto, directed by William Glassco, 2-4 February 1967. To these may be added the Oxford University Dramatic Society's production, directed by Clifford Williams of the Royal Shakespeare Company, 17-28 February 1970, which the *Oxford Times* found poorly acted in the main, but well produced, and another by the Adelaide Theatre Group, at the Sheridan Theatre, North Adelaide, directed by Alan Brissenden, 10 June (first of eleven performances) 1971. The second of these, which was the play's first Australian production, was presented uncut, on an open stage, in eighteenth-century dress. Critical opinion found it 'quite properly bawdy and enormously entertaining' (the *Advertiser*), and a reminder that 'preoccupation with sex is a characteristic not peculiar to the theatre today' (the *Sunday Mail*).

[28]See D. F. Rowan, 'The "Swan" Revisited', *Research Opportunities in Renaissance Drama*, X (1967), 33-48.

The first modern professional revival was directed by William Gaskill at the Royal Court Theatre, London, as part of a repertory season which began on 13 January 1966. The play was adapted by Edward Bond, whose play *Saved* was also in the season, and the costumes were flexibly modern, including Edwardian and contemporary dress. Gaskill was generally praised for the inventiveness of his production. Critical opinion ranged from the growling of the *Evening Standard*, 'Five plots—and it's still a bore' (a minority view), to the good sense of *The Times*, 'We could do with a modern Middleton', and the enthusiasm of the *Daily Express*, 'Rich in incident, and taken at a brisk, comic-strip pace, this production by the English Stage Company is witty, wise, and funny, and nobody should miss it'.

FURTHER READING

R. H. Barker, *Thomas Middleton*, New York, 1958.

M. C. Bradbrook, *The Growth and Structure of Elizabethan Comedy*, 1955.

R. Chatterji, 'Theme, Imagery and Unity in *A Chaste Maid in Cheapside*', *Renaissance Drama*, VIII (1965), 105–126.

U. M. Ellis-Fermor, *The Jacobean Drama*, revised edition, 1961.

D. M. Farr, *Thomas Middleton and the Drama of Realism*, Edinburgh, 1973, esp. pp. 23–37.

D. George, 'Thomas Middleton's Sources: A Survey', *N & Q*, XVIII (1971), 17–24.

C. Hallett, 'Middleton's Allwit: The Urban Cynic', *MLQ*, XXX (1969), 498–507.

D. M. Holmes, *The Art of Thomas Middleton*, Oxford, 1970.

L. C. Knights, *Drama and Society in the Age of Jonson*, 1962.

R. Levin, 'The Four Plots of *A Chaste Maid in Cheapside*', *RES*, N.S., XVI (1965), 14–24.

A. F. Marotti, 'Fertility and Comic Form in *A Chaste Maid in Cheapside*', *Comparative Drama*, III (1969), 65–74.

T. Middleton, *A Game at Chesse*, ed. R. C. Bald, Cambridge, 1929.

T. Middleton, *Hengist, King of Kent*, ed. R. C. Bald, New York, 1938.

T. Middleton, *A Chaste Maid in Cheapside*, ed. C. Barber, Edinburgh, 1969 (Fountainwell Drama Texts).

T. Middleton and S. Rowley, *The Changeling*, ed. N. W. Bawcutt, 1961 (Revels Plays).

T. Middleton, *A Chaste Maid in Cheapside*, ed. R. B. Parker, 1969 (Revels Plays).

R. B. Parker, 'Middleton's Experiments with Comedy and Judgement', in *Jacobean Theatre*, ed. J. R. Brown and B. Harris, 1960.

C. Ricks, 'Word-play in *Women Beware Women*', *RES*, N.S., XII (1961), 238–250.

S. Schoenbaum, *Middleton's Tragedies*, New York, 1955.

'*A Chaste Maid in Cheapside* and Middleton's City Comedy', in *Studies in the English Renaissance Drama*, ed. J. W. Bennett *et al.*, New York, 1959.

'*Hengist, King of Kent* and Sexual Preoccupation in Jacobean Drama', *PQ*, XXIX (1950), 182–198.

R. I. Williams, 'Machiavelli's *Mandragola*, Touchwood Senior, and the comedy of Middleton's *A Chaste Maid in Cheapside*', *SEL*, X (1970), 385–96.

Note. The place of publication of books mentioned throughout this edition is London unless stated otherwise.

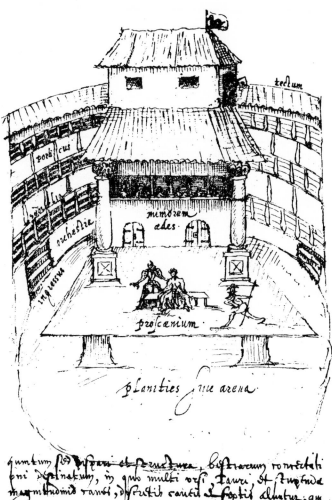

teflum

porticus

orchestra

mimorum
ædes

ingreſsus

proſcenium.

planities ſiue arena.

The de Witt sketch of the Swan Theatre c. 1596.
(Reproduced from the original in the Utrecht University Library,
MS 842, fol. 132ʳ.)

A

CHAST MAYD

ƒ ℵ

CHEAPE-SIDE.

A

Pleaſant conceited Comedy
neuer before printed.

As it hath beene often acted at the
Swan on the Banke-ſide, by the
Lady ELIZABETH her
Seruants.

By THOMAS MIDELTON Gent.

LONDON,
Printed for *Francis Constable* dwelling at the
ſigne of the *Crane* in *Pauls*
Church-yard.
1630.

9 *Swan* theatre stood in Paris Garden on the Bankside; built probably in 1596, used irregularly for plays and other entertainments until 1620 and still standing, though ruinous, in 1632. The inside was sketched by a Dutch visitor, Johannes de Witt, about 1596; a copy of this sketch, made by Arend van Buchell, was found in the Utrecht University Library and made known in 1888; it is the only known contemporary representation of an Elizabethan playhouse interior.

10-11 *Lady Elizabeth her Servants* were a company of adult players active 1611-16 in London, 1616-22 in the provinces, 1622-5 in London. Revived in 1628 as the Queen of Bohemia's Players, they continued until about 1641. The Lady Elizabeth was the eldest daughter of James I, born 1596, married Frederick V, Elector Palatine, 1613, became Queen of Bohemia 1619, died 1662.

15-16 *Paul's Churchyard* was the centre of the London book trade. 'The business premises around the cathedral church were of two classes, the houses which bordered the churchyards, and the less substantial booths (or lock-up shops) and stalls which clustered round the walls, and at the doors of the building itself' (H. G. Aldis, *C.H.E.L.*, IV (Cambridge, 1932), 398).

Title page of the quarto edition (reproduced by permission of the Huntington Library, San Marino, California).

The Names of the Principal Persons

MR YELLOWHAMMER, a goldsmith
MAUDLIN, his wife
TIM, their son
MOLL, their daughter
TUTOR to Tim   5
SIR WALTER WHOREHOUND, a suitor to Moll
SIR OLIVER KIX, and his WIFE, kin to Sir Walter
MR ALLWIT, and his WIFE, whom Sir Walter keeps
WELSH GENTLEWOMAN, Sir Walter's whore
WAT and NICK, his bastards [by Mrs Allwit]   10
DAVY DAHUMMA, his man
TOUCHWOOD SENIOR, and his WIFE, a decayed gentleman
TOUCHWOOD JUNIOR, another suitor to Moll
2 PROMOTERS
SERVANTS   15
WATERMEN
[PORTER   2 MEN, with baskets
GENTLEMAN   MISTRESS UNDERMAN, a Puritan
COUNTRY WENCH, with a child   PURITANS and GOSSIPS
JUGG, maid to Lady Kix   MIDWIFE   20
DRY NURSE   PARSON
WET NURSE   SUSAN, maid to Moll]

---

1 *Mr* contraction for 'Master', the more modern 'Mister' coming
  into general use later in the 17th century
7 *Kix* dry stem of a plant; *fig.* a sapless person. Middleton had
  used this name before in *A Trick to Catch the Old One* (*c.* 1605)
8 *Allwit* pun on 'wittol', a complacent cuckold
11 *Dahumma* from *dewch yma*, Welsh for 'come here'
12 *Touchwood* easily inflammable kindling

A CHASTE MAID IN CHEAPSIDE

Act I, [Scene i]

Enter MAUDLIN *and* MOLL, *a shop being discovered*

MAUDLIN

Have you played over all your old lessons o'the virginals?

MOLL

Yes.

MAUDLIN

Yes, you are a dull maid alate, methinks you had need have
somewhat to quicken your green sickness; do you weep? A
husband. Had not such a piece of flesh been ordained, what 5
had us wives been good for? To make salads, or else cried up
and down for samphire. To see the difference of these
seasons! When I was of your youth, I was lightsome, and
quick, two years before I was married. You fit for a knight's
bed—drowsy browed, dull eyed, drossy sprited—I hold my 10
life you have forgot your dancing: when was the dancer
with you?

MOLL

The last week.

MAUDLIN

Last week? When I was of your bord, he missed me not a
night, I was kept at it; I took delight to learn, and he to 15
teach me, pretty brown gentleman, he took pleasure in my
company; but you are dull, nothing comes nimbly from you,
you dance like a plumber's daughter, and deserve two

1 *virginals* popular keyboard instrument first mentioned in
England *c.* 1518; the strings are plucked, as in a spinet
4 *green sickness* chlorosis; anaemic disease mostly affecting young
women in puberty, giving them a pale or greenish complexion
10 *sprited* spirited   14 *bord* bore of a gun; 'when I was like you'

---

s.d. *discovered.* No 'discovery space' is shown on the de Witt sketch; this
direction, then, is possible evidence for a discovery area being built on
the stage when needed.
7 *samphire.* Plant growing on rocks by the sea, used in salads and especially good with marsh mutton. Wall suggests the sense here is 'we would
be reduced to being mere tit-bits for men'.
11 *dancing* was popular with all classes, and London dancing schools were a
sight for visitors; the sexual innuendo in Maudlin's reminiscences is plain.

thousand pounds in lead to your marriage, and not in
goldsmith's ware.   20

Enter YELLOWHAMMER

YELLOWHAMMER
Now what's the din betwixt mother and daughter, ha?
MAUDLIN
Faith small, telling your daughter Mary of her errors.
YELLOWHAMMER
'Errors', nay the city cannot hold you wife, but you must
needs fetch words from Westminster; I ha' done i'faith.
Has no attorney's clerk been here alate and changed his   25
half-crown-piece his mother sent him, or rather cozened you
with a gilded twopence, to bring the word in fashion for her
faults or cracks in duty and obedience, term 'em e'en so,
sweet wife? As there is no woman made without a flaw,
your purest lawns have frays, and cambrics bracks.   30
MAUDLIN
But 'tis a husband solders up all cracks.
MOLL
What is he come sir?
YELLOWHAMMER
Sir Walter's come.
He was met at Holborn Bridge, and in his company
A proper fair young gentlewoman, which I guess   35
By her red hair, and other rank descriptions,
To be his landed niece brought out of Wales,
Which Tim our son (the Cambridge boy) must marry.

26 *half-crown-piece* made of 22 carat gold, struck only in last
   coinage of Henry VIII and one coinage of Elizabeth
27 *twopence* made of silver, as were all coins worth a shilling or less
30 *lawn* fine linen or clothing made from it; so called because it was
   bleached on a lawn instead of the ordinary bleaching grounds
30 *cambrics* a kind of fine white linen, originally made at Cambray in
   France, or clothing made from it
30 *brack* flaw, fault, opening. This whole passage is innuendo
36 *rank* an intensitive, but here there may be a pun on the meaning
   'coarse'

24 *Westminster* where justice was dispensed; Henry III ordered that the
   great hall at Westminster should be 'the usual place of pleadings, and
   ministration of justice' (*Survey*, II, 117). Yellowhammer is saying, 'Has
   no attorney's clerk from Westminster been here lately to bribe you into
   using a highfalutin word (errors) for your daughter's faults? Isn't the
   ordinary language of the City good enough for you?'
34 *Holborn Bridge*, ancient bridge of London, over the Fleet Ditch.

'Tis a match of Sir Walter's own making
To bind us to him, and our heirs for ever.   40

MAUDLIN
We are honoured then, if this baggage would be humble, and
    kiss him with devotion when he enters.
I cannot get her for my life
To instruct her hand thus, before and after,
Which a knight will look for, before and after.   45
I have told her still, 'tis the waving of a woman
Does often move a man, and prevails strongly.
But sweet, ha' you sent to Cambridge,
Has Tim word on't?

YELLOWHAMMER
Had word just the day after when you sent him the silver   50
    spoon to eat his broth in the hall, amongst the gentlemen
    commoners.

MAUDLIN
O 'twas timely.
                        Enter PORTER

YELLOWHAMMER
How now?

PORTER
A letter from a gentleman in Cambridge.   55

YELLOWHAMMER
O, one of Hobson's porters, thou art welcome. I told thee
Maud we should hear from Tim. *Amantissimis charissimisque
ambobus parentibus patri et matri.*

---

44 *her hand* to learn ladylike gestures; innuendo in 'before and after'
46 *still* constantly
51 *hall* dining hall shared by students and members of a college

---

51–52 *gentlemen commoners.* A privileged class of undergraduates at
    Oxford and Cambridge, who wore a special gown and velvet cap, dined
    at a separate table and paid higher fees.
56 *Hobson* (1544?–1631), the famous carrier of Cambridge who gave no
    alternative choice to those hiring his horses and so gave rise to the
    phrase 'Hobson's choice' (though this has been held to be a Cambridge
    hoax); from 1570 to 1630 his large 6 and 8 horse wagons carried goods
    and mail between Cambridge and London; he died very rich and
    Milton wrote two epitaphs for him.
57–58 'To my most loving and dearest parents, both father and mother'.
    Dyce and Bullen correct the Latin throughout the play, but as in some
    places the grammatical mistakes indicate a greater foolishness the
    original has been retained in this edition although the spelling has been
    modernized.

MAUDLIN

What's the matter?

YELLOWHAMMER

Nay by my troth, I know not, ask not me, he's grown too   60
verbal; this learning is a great witch.

MAUDLIN

Pray let me see it, I was wont to understand him. *Aman-
tissimus charissimus*, he has sent the carrier's man, he says:
ambobus parentibus, for a pair of boots: *patri et matri*, pay
the porter, or it makes no matter.   65

PORTER

Yes by my faith mistress, there's no true construction in
that, I have took a great deal of pains, and come from the
Bell sweating. Let me come to't, for I was a scholar forty
years ago; 'tis thus I warrant you: *Matri*, it makes no
matter: *ambobus parentibus*, for a pair of boots: *patri* pay   70
the porter: *amantissimis charissimis*, he's the carrier's man,
and his name is Sims, and there he says true, forsooth
my name is Sims indeed; I have not forgot all my learning.
A money matter, I thought I should hit on't.

YELLOWHAMMER

Go thou art an old fox, there's a tester for thee.   75

PORTER

If I see your worship at Goose Fair, I have a dish of birds
for you.

YELLOWHAMMER

Why, dost dwell at Bow?

PORTER

All my lifetime sir I could ever say Bo, to a goose.
Farewell to your worship.   *Exit* PORTER   80

YELLOWHAMMER

A merry porter.

59 *matter* content
75 *tester* sixpence (sl.). First applied to the shilling of Henry VII but
this became debased and the value fell
76 *Goose Fair* held annually on the Thursday after Pentecost at
Stratford le Bow, $4\frac{1}{2}$ miles northeast of St Paul's
76 *dish of birds* geese were roasted and sold at the Fair; 'bird' was
also sl. for a woman.
79 *Bo, to a goose* proverbial. In Hollar's panorama of London (1647)
Bow Church in the city is labelled 'Boo'

68 *Bell*. Almost certainly a misprint for 'Bull', the inn on the western side
of Bishopsgate which was Hobson's place of call.

MAUDLIN

How can he choose but be so, coming with Cambridge
letters from our son Tim?

YELLOWHAMMER

What's here? *Maximus diligo*. Faith I must to my learned
counsel with this gear, 'twill ne'er be discerned else.   85

MAUDLIN

Go to my cousin then, at Inns of Court.

YELLOWHAMMER

Fie, they are all for French, they speak no Latin.

MAUDLIN

The parson then will do it.

Enter a GENTLEMAN *with a chain.*

YELLOWHAMMER

Nay he disclaims it, calls Latin Papistry, he will not deal
with it. What is't you lack gentleman?   90

GENTLEMAN

Pray weigh this chain.

Enter SIR WALTER WHOREHOUND, WELSH GENTLEWOMAN
and DAVY DAHUMMA

SIR WALTER

Now wench thou art welcome to the heart of the city of
London.

WELSH GENTLEWOMAN

Dugat a whee.

SIR WALTER

You can thank me in English if you list.   95

WELSH GENTLEWOMAN

I can sir simply.

SIR WALTER

'Twill serve to pass wench; 'twas strange that I should lie
with thee so often, to leave thee without English—that

---

85 *gear* matter, stuff   91 s.d. *Dahumma* (Dahanna Q)

---

84 'I esteem you most highly'.
86 *Inns of Court.* Houses of law students, 'a whole University, as it were, of
   students, practisers or pleaders and Judges of the laws' (*Survey*, I, 76);
   Lincoln's Inn, Gray's Inn, the Inner Temple and the Middle Temple
   were the most important of the fourteen in 1603.
87 *French.* The mongrel language known as 'Law French' continued in
   use for centuries in England; finally abolished by an act of Parliament
   in 1731.
94 'God preserve you'—a phonetic rendering of '*Duw cadw chwi*'

were unnatural. I bring thee up to turn thee into gold
wench, and make thy fortune shine like your bright trade.   100
A goldsmith's shop sets out a city maid. Davy Dahumma, not
a word.

DAVY
Mum, mum sir.

SIR WALTER
Here you must pass for a pure virgin.

DAVY
[*Aside*] Pure Welsh virgin, she lost her maidenhead in   105
Brecknockshire.

SIR WALTER
I hear you mumble Davy.

DAVY
I have teeth sir, I need not mumble yet this forty years.

SIR WALTER
The knave bites plaguily.

YELLOWHAMMER
What's your price sir?   110

GENTLEMAN
A hundred pound sir.

YELLOWHAMMER
A hundred marks the utmost, 'tis not for me else.
                                        [*Exit* GENTLEMAN]
What, Sir Walter Whorehound?

MOLL
O death.   *Exit* MOLL

MAUDLIN
Why daughter;   115
Faith, the baggage,
A bashful girl sir; these young things are shamefast,
Besides you have a presence, sweet Sir Walter,
Able to daunt a maid brought up i'the city;

Enter MOLL

A brave Court spirit makes our virgins quiver,   120
And kiss with trembling thighs. Yet see she comes sir.

103 *Mum* cant term, sign of silence and secrecy
112 *marks* 1 mark = 13s 4d
117 *shamefast* bashful, modest   119 s.d. MOLL ed. (Mary Q)

---

106 *Brecknockshire*. Welsh county, probably chosen here because 'nock' was
   one of the many sl. words for the female genitals.
121 *trembling thighs*. A plain reference to the lasciviousness of the Court; a
   'knee-trembler' was coitus in a standing position. Romeo's Rosaline had
   a 'trembling thigh' (*Romeo and Juliet*, II, i, 19).

SIR WALTER

Why how now pretty mistress, now I have caught you.
What, can you injure so your time to stray thus from your
faithful servant?

YELLOWHAMMER

Pish, stop your words good knight, 'twill make her blush 125
else, which sound too high for the daughters of the freedom. 'Honour', and 'faithful servant', they are compliments
for the worthies of Whitehall, or Greenwich. E'en plain,
sufficient subsidy words serves us sir. And is this gentlewoman your worthy niece? 130

SIR WALTER

You may be bold with her on these terms, 'tis she sir, heir
to some nineteen mountains.

YELLOWHAMMER

Bless us all, you overwhelm me sir with love and riches.

SIR WALTER

And all as high as Paul's.

DAVY

Here's work i'faith. 135

SIR WALTER

How sayst thou Davy?

DAVY

Higher sir by far, you cannot see the top of 'em.

YELLOWHAMMER

What man? Maudlin salute this gentlewoman, our daughter
if things hit right.

Enter TOUCHWOOD JUNIOR

TOUCHWOOD JUNIOR

My knight with a brace of footmen 140
Is come and brought up his ewe mutton
To find a ram at London; I must hasten it,

---

126 *sound* ed. (wound Q); *daughters of the freedom* of the city as opposed to the court 129 *subsidy* business, commercial, as opposed
to courtly 138 *salute* kiss 141 *ewe mutton* old strumpet

---

128 *Whitehall*. A royal palace from 1529 when Henry VIII took it from
Wolsey; east of Westminster.

128 *Greenwich*. Ancient royal palace on the south bank of the Thames below
London; birthplace of Henry VIII, Mary I and Elizabeth I.

134 *as high as Paul's* was proverbial; the cathedral tower was 245 feet, the
steeple which surmounted it for another 205 feet was destroyed by fire
in 1561.

Or else pick a famine; her blood's mine,
And that's the surest. Well knight, that choice spoil
Is only kept for me.   145

MOLL
    Sir?

TOUCHWOOD JUNIOR
    Turn not to me till thou mayst lawfully, it but whets my
    stomach, which is too sharp set already. Read that note
    carefully, keep me from suspicion still, nor know my zeal
    but in thy heart: read and send but thy liking in three   150
    words, I'll be at hand to take it.

YELLOWHAMMER
    O Tim sir, Tim.
    A poor plain boy, an university man,
    Proceeds next Lent to a Bachelor of Art;
    He will be called Sir Yellowhammer then   155
    Over all Cambridge, and that's half a knight.

MAUDLIN
    Please you draw near, and taste the welcome of the city sir?

YELLOWHAMMER
    Come good Sir Walter, and your virtuous niece here.

SIR WALTER
    'Tis manners to take kindness.

YELLOWHAMMER
    Lead 'em in wife.   160

SIR WALTER
    Your company sir.

YELLOWHAMMER
    I'll give't you instantly.
            [*Exeunt* SIR WALTER, WELSH GENTLEWOMAN, DAVY *and*
                                                MAUDLIN]

TOUCHWOOD JUNIOR
    How strangely busy is the devil and riches;
    Poor soul kept in too hard, her mother's eye

---

143 *pick a famine* choose a famine. (Ed. incorrectly emend 'peak
    a'famine', i.e. 'dwindle from starvation')
143 *blood* passion (but also with a hunting connotation here)
144 *spoil* ed. (spoy Q)   148 *sharp set* eager, keen   152 *Tim* ed. (Turn Q)
148 *sharp set* eager, keen
154 *Proceeds* graduates (strictly, to a degree higher than Bachelor)

---

154 *Art.* Could signify Yellowhammer's ignorance, but Dekker uses 'Bachelor
    of Art' without humorous intent in *The Gull's Hornbook* (1609, p. 9).
155 *Sir Yellowhammer.* 'Sir' was a rendering of *dominus* to indicate a B.A. of
    Oxford and Cambridge; students were considered as gentry.

Is cruel toward her, being to him.   165
'Twere a good mirth now to set him awork
To make her wedding ring. I must about it.
Rather than the gain should fall to a stranger,
'Twas honesty in me to enrich my father.

YELLOWHAMMER

The girl is wondrous peevish; I fear nothing   170
But that she's taken with some other love,
Then all's quite dashed; that must be narrowly looked to;
We cannot be too wary in our children.
What is't you lack?

TOUCHWOOD JUNIOR

O nothing now, all that I wish is present. I would have a   175
wedding ring made for a gentlewoman, with all speed that
may be.

YELLOWHAMMER

Of what weight sir?

TOUCHWOOD JUNIOR

Of some half ounce, stand fair and comely, with the spark
of a diamond. Sir 'twere pity to lose the least grace.   180

YELLOWHAMMER

Pray let's see it; indeed sir 'tis a pure one.

TOUCHWOOD JUNIOR

So is the mistress.

YELLOWHAMMER

Have you the wideness of her finger sir?

TOUCHWOOD JUNIOR

Yes sure I think I have her measure about me—
Good faith 'tis down, I cannot show't you,   185
I must pull too many things out to be certain.
Let me see, long, and slender, and neatly jointed,
Just such another gentlewoman that's your daughter sir.

YELLOWHAMMER

And therefore sir no gentlewoman.

TOUCHWOOD JUNIOR

I protest I never saw two maids handed more alike;   190
I'll ne'er seek farther, if you'll give me leave sir.

185 *down* lost

---

165 *being to him.* Turned to Whorehound, supporting Yellowhammer in
arranging for Moll to marry the knight.
180 *diamond.* Wedding rings were often in the form of two hands clasping a
heart made of a jewel, or a hoop, sometimes enamelled. with small
gems, and a posy engraved inside.

YELLOWHAMMER
> If you dare venture by her finger sir.

TOUCHWOOD JUNIOR
> Ay, and I'll bide all loss sir.

YELLOWHAMMER
> Say you so sir, let's see hither girl.

TOUCHWOOD JUNIOR
> Shall I make bold with your finger gentlewoman?   195

MOLL
> Your pleasure sir.

TOUCHWOOD JUNIOR
> That fits her to a hair sir.

YELLOWHAMMER
> What's your posy now sir?

TOUCHWOOD JUNIOR
> Mass that's true, posy i'faith, e'en thus sir:
> Love that's wise, blinds parents' eyes.   200

YELLOWHAMMER
> How, how? If I may speak without offence sir,
> I hold my life—

TOUCHWOOD JUNIOR
> What sir?

YELLOWHAMMER
> Go to, you'll pardon me?

TOUCHWOOD JUNIOR
> Pardon you? Ay sir.   205

YELLOWHAMMER
> Will you i'faith?

TOUCHWOOD JUNIOR
> Yes faith I will.

YELLOWHAMMER
> You'll steal away some man's daughter, am I near you?
> Do you turn aside? You gentlemen are mad wags; I wonder
> things can be so warily carried,   210
> And parents blinded so, but they're served right
> That have two eyes, and wear so dull a sight.

TOUCHWOOD JUNIOR
> [*Aside*] Thy doom take hold of thee.

198 *posy* a motto, originally a line of verse or 'poesie', inscribed inside
a ring
199 *Mass* 'by the Mass', an oath
212 *wear* (were Q) ed. emend 'were so dull a'sight', but cf. IV, ii, 36
for a similar use of this spelling in Q

YELLOWHAMMER

Tomorrow noon shall show your ring well done.

TOUCHWOOD JUNIOR

Being so 'tis soon; thanks, and your leave sweet gentle-   215
  woman.   *Exit*

MOLL

Sir you are welcome.

[*Aside*] O were I made of wishes, I went with thee.

YELLOWHAMMER

Come now we'll see how the rules go within.

MOLL

That robs my joy, there I lose all I win.   *Ex*[*eunt*] 220

[Act I, Scene ii]

Enter DAVY *and* ALLWIT *severally*

DAVY

Honesty wash my eyes, I have spied a wittol.

ALLWIT

What, Davy Dahumma? Welcome from North Wales
I'faith, and is Sir Walter come?

DAVY

New come to town sir.

ALLWIT

Into the maids sweet Davy, and give order his chamber   5
be made ready instantly; my wife's as great as she can
wallow Davy, and longs for nothing but pickled cucumbers,
and his coming, and now she shall ha't boy.

DAVY

She's sure of them sir.

ALLWIT

Thy very sight will hold my wife in pleasure, till the knight   10
come himself. Go in, in, in Davy.   *Exit* [DAVY]
The founder's come to town; I am like a man
Finding a table furnished to his hand,
As mine is still to me, prays for the founder;
Bless the right worshipful, the good founder's life.   15

---

219 *rules* unruly behaviour; 'Tumultuous frolicsome conduct'
  (J. O. Halliwell, *Dictionary of Archaic and Provincial Words*
  (1874))

---

7 *pickled cucumbers*. Made with verjuice, a sharp cider, rather than
  vinegar, milder than modern pickles; pregnancy produces strange
  cravings.

I thank him, h'as maintained my house this ten years,
Not only keeps my wife, but a keeps me,
And all my family; I am at his table,
He gets me all my children, and pays the nurse,
Monthly, or weekly, puts me to nothing,   20
Rent, nor church duties, not so much as the scavenger:
The happiest state that ever man was born to.
I walk out in a morning, come to breakfast,
Find excellent cheer, a good fire in winter,
Look in my coal house about midsummer eve,   25
That's full, five or six chaldron, new laid up;
Look in my back yard, I shall find a steeple
Made up with Kentish faggots, which o'erlooks
The waterhouse and the windmills; I say nothing
But smile, and pin the door. When she lies in,   30
As now she's even upon the point of grunting,
A lady lies not in like her; there's her embossings,
Embroiderings, spanglings, and I know not what,
As if she lay with all the gaudy shops
In Gresham's Burse about her; then her restoratives,   35
Able to set up a young 'pothecary,
And richly stock the foreman of a drug shop;
Her sugar by whole loaves, her wines by rundlets.
I see these things, but like a happy man,

17 *a* he
18 *family* includes servants as well as children
38 *rundlets* small barrels; large rundlets held between 12 and 18½
gallons, small between a pint and four gallons

---

21 *scavenger.* Officer of the town who employed the poor to sweep the street;
Stow says Bread St. ward, which contained part of Cheapside, had eight.
26 *chaldron.* A dry measure of 36 bushels of coal; the coal trade between
Newcastle and London grew tenfold between 1545 and 1625 and while
Shakespeare was in London the price per chaldron rose from four
shillings to nine.
28 *Kentish faggots.* Bundles of brushwood, about eight feet long and one
foot through; much London firewood came from Kent.
29 *waterhouse and the windmills.* Built near Broken Wharf in 1594 by
Bevis Bulmer 'to convey Thames water into men's houses of West
Cheap, about Paul's, Fleet Street, &c' (*Survey*, I, 8). Visscher's *View of
London* (1616) shows the waterhouse with a windmill on the top.
35 *Gresham's Burse.* The Royal Exchange, 'whose founder was Sir Thomas
Gresham Knight, agent to her Majesty, built 1566–8 for the con-
fluence and commerce of merchants' (John Speed, *The Theatre of . . .
Great Britain* (1611), fol. 852).

I pay for none at all, yet fools think's mine;   40
I have the name, and in his gold I shine.
And where some merchants would in soul kiss hell,
To buy a paradise for their wives, and dye
Their conscience in the bloods of prodigal heirs,
To deck their night-piece, yet all this being done,   45
Eaten with jealousy to the inmost bone—
As what affliction nature more constrains,
Than feed the wife plump for another's veins?—
These torments stand I freed of, I am as clear
From jealousy of a wife as from the charge.   50
O two miraculous blessings; 'tis the knight
Hath took that labour all out of my hands;
I may sit still and play; he's jealous for me—
Watches her steps, sets spies—I live at ease;
He has both the cost and torment; when the strings   55
Of his heart frets, I feed, laugh, or sing,
La dildo, dildo la dildo, la dildo dildo de dildo.

Enter two SERVANTS

1 SERVANT
What has he got asinging in his head now?
2 SERVANT
Now's out of work he falls to making dildoes.
ALLWIT
Now sirs, Sir Walter's come.   60
1 SERVANT
Is our master come?
ALLWIT
Your master? What am I?

40 *think's* think it's
45 *night-piece* mistress, bedfellow
57 *dildo* chorus with ironic overtones since a dildo is a substitute
   phallus
58 *asinging . . . head* reference to cuckold's horns
59 *work* sexual activity (sl.)

43–44 *dye their conscience . . . heirs.* 'Wickedly extort money from spend-
thrift sons of the gentry to buy clothing and jewellery for their whores'.
Gulling 'prodigal heirs' is a major theme in Middleton's *Michaelmas
Term* (*c.* 1606).
55–56 *strings . . . frets.* The heart was supposed to be braced with strings,
which frayed and broke under emotional stress; the fret of a musical
instrument was a ring of gut, now wood or metal, on the fingerboard to
regulate fingering.

1 SERVANT
Do not you know sir?
ALLWIT
Pray am not I your master?
1 SERVANT
O you are but our mistress's husband.   65

                Enter SIR WALTER *and* DAVY
ALLWIT
Ergo knave, your master.
1 SERVANT
Negatur argumentum. Here comes Sir Walter, now a stands
bare as well as we; make the most of him he's but one peep
above a servingman, and so much his horns make him.
SIR WALTER
How dost Jack?   70
ALLWIT
Proud of your worship's health sir.
SIR WALTER
How does your wife?
ALLWIT
E'en after your own making sir,
She's a tumbler i'faith, the nose and belly meets.
SIR WALTER
They'll part in time again.   75
ALLWIT
At the good hour, they will, and please your worship.
SIR WALTER
Here sirrah, pull off my boots. Put on, put on Jack.
ALLWIT
I thank your kind worship sir.
SIR WALTER
Slippers! Heart, you are sleepy.
ALLWIT
The game begins already.   80
SIR WALTER
Pish, put on Jack.

---

69 *horns* the common insignia of the cuckold
77 *Put on* Allwit has deferentially taken off his hat

---

66 'Therefore'.
67 'Your argument is denied'.
68 *peep.* Pip, degree; from a card game 'one-and-thirty' in which thirty-two
   was 'a pip out', the pips being the spots on the cards.

ALLWIT
  Now I must do it, or he'll be as angry now as if I had put
  it on at first bidding; 'tis but observing, 'tis but observing
  a man's humour once, and he may ha' him by the nose all
  his life.   85

SIR WALTER
  What entertainment has lain open here?
  No strangers in my absence?

1 SERVANT
  Sure sir not any.

ALLWIT
  His jealousy begins, am not I happy now
  That can laugh inward whilst his marrow melts?   90

SIR WALTER
  How do you satisfy me?

1 SERVANT
  Good sir be patient.

SIR WALTER
  For two months' absence I'll be satisfied.

1 SERVANT
  No living creature entered—

SIR WALTER
  Entered? Come swear—   95

1 SERVANT
  You will not hear me out sir—

SIR WALTER
  Yes I'll hear't out sir.

1 SERVANT
  Sir he can tell himself.

SIR WALTER   Heart he can tell!
  Do you think I'll trust him? As a usurer
  With forfeited lordships. Him, O monstrous injury!   100
  Believe him? Can the devil speak ill of darkness?
  What can you say sir?

ALLWIT
  Of my soul and conscience sir, she's a wife as honest of her
  body to me as any lord's proud lady can be.

SIR WALTER
  Yet, by your leave, I heard you were once offering to go to   105
  bed to her.

84 *he* one, you

---

90 *marrow melts*. With the heat generated by his jealousy.
100 *forfeited lordships*. A jibe at the low value of knighthood.

ALLWIT
  No I protest sir.

SIR WALTER
  Heart if you do, you shall take all—I'll marry.

ALLWIT
  O I beseech you sir—

SIR WALTER
  That wakes the slave, and keeps his flesh in awe.   110

ALLWIT
  I'll stop that gap
  Where e'er I find it open; I have poisoned
  His hopes in marriage already—
  Some old rich widows, and some landed virgins—

Enter two CHILDREN

  And I'll fall to work still before I'll lose him,   115
  He's yet too sweet to part from.

1 BOY
  God-den father.

ALLWIT
  Ha villain, peace.

2 BOY
  God-den father.

ALLWIT
  Peace bastard; should he hear 'em! These are two foolish   120
  children, they do not know the gentleman that sits there.

SIR WALTER
  Oh Wat, how dost Nick? Go to school,
  Ply your books boys, ha?

ALLWIT
  Where's your legs whoresons? They should kneel indeed if
  they could say their prayers.   125

SIR WALTER
  Let me see, stay,
  How shall I dispose of these two brats now
  When I am married, for they must not mingle
  Amongst my children that I get in wedlock,
  'Twill make foul work that, and raise many storms.   130
  I'll bind Wat prentice to a goldsmith, my father Yellow-
    hammer;

117 *God-den* 'good evening', but used any time after noon

124 *legs*. A bow; cf. *The Revenger's Tragedy* IV, ii, 41, '[Vindice] snatches off
  his hat, and makes legs to him'.

As fit as can be. Nick with some vintner, good, goldsmith
And vintner; there will be wine in bowls, i'faith.

Enter ALLWIT'S WIFE

MISTRESS ALLWIT
    Sweet knight   135
    Welcome; I have all my longings now in town,
    Now well-come the good hour.
SIR WALTER
    How cheers my mistress?
MISTRESS ALLWIT
    Made lightsome, e'en by him that made me heavy.
SIR WALTER
    Methinks she shows gallantly, like a moon at full sir.   140
ALLWIT
    True, and if she bear a male child, there's the man in the
    moon sir.
SIR WALTER
    'Tis but the boy in the moon yet goodman calf.
ALLWIT
    There was a man, the boy had never been there else.
SIR WALTER
    It shall be yours sir.   145
                [*Exeunt* MISTRESS ALLWIT *and* SIR WALTER]
ALLWIT
    No by my troth, I'll swear it's none of mine, let him that
    got it keep it. Thus do I rid myself of fear,
    Lie soft, sleep hard, drink wine, and eat good cheer. [*Exit*]

Act II, [Scene i]

Enter TOUCHWOOD SENIOR *and his* WIFE

MISTRESS TOUCHWOOD
    'Twill be so tedious sir to live from you,
    But that necessity must be obeyed.
TOUCHWOOD SENIOR
    I would it might not wife, the tediousness
    Will be the most part mine, that understand
    The blessings I have in thee; so to part,   5
    That drives the torment to a knowing heart;
    But as thou sayst, we must give way to need

---

143 *calf*. Blockhead. Another small but subtle irony, since a 'mooncalf' is
   also a false pregnancy.

And live awhile asunder, our desires
Are both too fruitful for our barren fortunes.
How adverse runs the destiny of some creatures—   10
Some only can get riches and no children,
We only can get children and no riches;
Then 'tis the prudent'st part to check our wills,
And till our state rise, make our bloods lie still.
Life every year a child, and some years two,   15
Besides drinkings abroad, that's never reckoned;
This gear will not hold out.

MISTRESS TOUCHWOOD
Sir for a time, I'll take the courtesy of my uncle's house
If you be pleased to like on't, till prosperity
Look with a friendly eye upon our states.   20

TOUCHWOOD SENIOR
Honest wife I thank thee; I ne'er knew
The perfect treasure thou brought'st with thee more
Than at this instant minute. A man's happy
When he's at poorest that has matched his soul
As rightly as his body. Had I married   25
A sensual fool now, as 'tis hard to 'scape it
'Mongst gentlewomen of our time, she would ha' hanged
About my neck, and never left her hold
Till she had kissed me into wanton businesses,
Which at the waking of my better judgement   30
I should have cursed most bitterly,
And laid a thicker vengeance on my act
Than misery of the birth, which were enough
If it were born to greatness, whereas mine
Is sure of beggary, though it were got in wine.   35
Fulness of joy showeth the goodness in thee,
Thou art a matchless wife; farewell my joy.

MISTRESS TOUCHWOOD
I shall not want your sight?

TOUCHWOOD SENIOR   I'll see thee often,
Talk in mirth, and play at kisses with thee,

13 *wills* sexual desires
14 *bloods* passions
17 *gear* business, with a pun on the sl. meaning 'genitals'

15 *Life*. God's life. An Act for the 'preventing . . . of the great abuse of the
Holy Name of God in Stage plays, interludes . . . and such like' was
passed in May 1606; offenders were liable for a fine of £10 for each
lapse.

Anything wench but what may beget beggars;   40
There I give o'er the set, throw down the cards,
And dare not take them up.
MISTRESS TOUCHWOOD   Your will be mine sir.   *Exit*
TOUCHWOOD SENIOR
This does not only make her honesty perfect,
But her discretion, and approves her judgement.
Had her desires been wanton, they'd been blameless   45
In being lawful ever, but of all creatures
I hold that wife a most unmatched treasure
That can unto her fortunes fix her pleasure,
And not unto her blood—this is like wedlock;
The feast of marriage is not lust but love,   50
And care of the estate. When I please blood,
Merely I sing, and suck out others'; then,
'Tis many a wise man's fault; but of all men
I am the most unfortunate in that game
That ever pleased both genders, I ne'er played yet   55
Under a bastard; the poor wenches curse me
To the pit where e'er I come; they were ne'er served so,
But used to have more words than one to a bargain.
I have such a fatal finger in such business
I must forth with't, chiefly for country wenches,   60
For every harvest I shall hinder hay-making;

Enter a WENCH *with a child*

I had no less than seven lay in last Progress,
Within three weeks of one another's time.
WENCH
O Snaphance, have I found you?

41 *set* game, as in tennis
45 *desires* ed. (desire Q)
52 *merely . . . others'* my slightest sexual activity always hurts
   somebody

---

52 *sing.* Have sexual intercourse with (See E. Partridge, *Shakespeare's Bawdy* (1956), p. 187).
57 *pit.* Hell, with a sexual pun continued throughout the next five lines with 'served', 'words' and 'finger'; the girls are not used to becoming pregnant after only one sexual episode.
62 *Progress.* Annual royal visit to various parts of the country, usually in July and August; expensive festivities and a holiday atmosphere were expected by the sovereign.
64 *Snaphance.* Flintlock on guns, or, more appropriately here, a musket or gun fitted with a flintlock.

TOUCHWOOD SENIOR   How Snaphance?
WENCH
   Do you see your workmanship?   65
   Nay turn not from it, nor offer to escape, for if you do,
   I'll cry it through the streets, and follow you.
   Your name may well be called Touchwood, a pox on you,
   You do but touch and take; thou hast undone me;
   I was a maid before, I can bring a certificate for it,   70
   From both the churchwardens.
TOUCHWOOD SENIOR
   I'll have the parson's hand too, or I'll not yield to't.
WENCH
   Thou shalt have more thou villain; nothing grieves me, but
   Ellen my poor cousin in Derbyshire, thou hast cracked her
   marriage quite; she'll have a bout with thee.   75
TOUCHWOOD SENIOR
   Faith when she will I'll have a bout with her.
WENCH
   A law bout sir I mean.
TOUCHWOOD SENIOR
   True, lawyers use such bouts as other men do,
   And if that be all thy grief, I'll tender her a husband;
   I keep of purpose two or three gulls in pickle   80
   To eat such mutton with, and she shall choose one.
   Do but in courtesy faith wench excuse me
   Of this half yard of flesh, in which I think it wants
   A nail or two.
WENCH   No, thou shalt find villain
   It hath right shape, and all the nails it should have.   85
TOUCHWOOD SENIOR
   Faith I am poor; do a charitable deed wench,

---

83 *half yard of flesh* the baby, but perhaps with pun on sl. for phallus
84 *nail* a measure of cloth, one sixteenth of a yard; here with a pun on
    fingernail, as the children of syphilitics were sometimes born
    without nails

---

71 *churchwardens.* Lay honorary officers who helped the incumbent of a
    parish; they could issue a character reference, though these were not
    reliable (cf. 'a certificate (such as Rogues have) from the head men of
    the Parish', Thomas Nashe, *Strange News* (1592), sig. C4ᵛ).
75 *bout.* Quarrel; taken up by Touchwood Senior in the sexual sense and
    used again in the legal sense.
80–81 *gulls . . . one.* 'I keep a few fools for such whores and she can have
    one for a husband'. 'In pickle' also has the meaning 'poxed'.

I am a younger brother, and have nothing.

WENCH
Nothing! Thou hast too much thou lying villain
Unless thou wert more thankful.

TOUCHWOOD SENIOR   I have no dwelling,
I brake up house but this morning; pray thee pity me,   90
I am a good fellow, faith have been too kind
To people of your gender; if I ha't
Without my belly, none of your sex shall want it;
That word has been of force to move a woman.
There's tricks enough to rid thy hand on't wench,   95
Some rich man's porch, tomorrow before day,
Or else anon i'the evening—twenty devices;
Here's all I have, i'faith, take purse and all,
And would I were rid of all the ware i'the shop so.

WENCH
Where I find manly dealings I am pitiful,   100
This shall not trouble you.

TOUCHWOOD SENIOR
And I protest wench, the next I'll keep myself.

WENCH
Soft, let it be got first.
This is the fifth; if e'er I venture more
Where I now go for a maid, may I ride for a whore.   *Exit*   105

TOUCHWOOD SENIOR
What shift she'll make now with this piece of flesh
In this strict time of Lent, I cannot imagine;
Flesh dare not peep abroad now; I have known
This city now above this seven years,
But I protest in better state of government   110
I never knew it yet, nor ever heard of;
There has been more religious wholesome laws

95 *on't* of it
105 *ride* be carted as a whore through the streets to prison; also to
    copulate

---

87 *younger brother*. The custom of primogeniture, by which property and
   title descended to the first born, meant that younger sons often had to
   live by their wits.
92–93 *if I . . . want it*. Either, 'while I have a phallus, no woman shall
   lack it' or 'if I have it without my appetite then none of you will desire
   it'; a puzzling passage.
99 *ware i'the shop*. All my other bastards; also, perhaps, all other female
   temptation, as 'ware' is sl. for female privities.
107 *Lent*. See Introduction pp. xiii, xxi.

In the half circle of a year erected
For common good, than memory ever knew of,

Enter SIR OLIVER KIX *and his* LADY

Setting apart corruption of promoters,   115
And other poisonous officers that infect
And with a venomous breath taint every goodness.
LADY KIX
O that e'er I was begot, or bred, or born.
SIR OLIVER
Be content sweet wife.
TOUCHWOOD SENIOR   What's here to do now?
I hold my life she's in deep passion   120
For the imprisonment of veal and mutton
Now kept in garrets, weeps for some calf's head now;
Methinks her husband's head might serve with bacon.

Enter TOUCHWOOD JUNIOR

LADY KIX
Hist.
SIR OLIVER
Patience sweet wife.   125
TOUCHWOOD JUNIOR
Brother I have sought you strangely.
TOUCHWOOD SENIOR
Why what's the business?
TOUCHWOOD JUNIOR
With all speed thou canst, procure a licence for me.
TOUCHWOOD SENIOR
How, a licence?
TOUCHWOOD JUNIOR
Cud's foot she's lost else, I shall miss her ever.   130

122 *calf's head* also means a fool
126 *strangely* extremely; 'I've been looking hard for you'
130 *Cud's foot* a defanged oath

---

115 *promoter*. Originally a lawyer, but by 1600 an informer; in Lent the
    authorities had promoters spying for butchers who sold meat without a
    licence.
124 *Hist*. Ed. give this to Touchwood Junior but as it means 'Be quiet!' it is
    appropriate for Lady Kix, as in Q.
128 *licence*. Only the Archbishop of Canterbury could issue a licence for a
    marriage in a place other than a church or chapel; a licence was also
    necessary for a marriage for which banns had not been called.

TOUCHWOOD SENIOR
   Nay sure thou shalt not miss so fair a mark
   For thirteen shillings fourpence.

TOUCHWOOD JUNIOR   Thanks by hundreds.
                Exit [with TOUCHWOOD SENIOR]

SIR OLIVER
   Nay pray thee cease, I'll be at more cost yet,
   Thou know'st we are rich enough.

LADY KIX   All but in blessings,
   And there the beggar goes beyond us. O, O, O,   135
   To be seven years a wife and not a child, O not a child!

SIR OLIVER
   Sweet wife have patience.

LADY KIX
   Can any woman have a greater cut?

SIR OLIVER
   I know 'tis great, but what of that wife?
   I cannot do withal; there's things making   140
   By thine own doctor's advice at 'pothecary's;
   I spare for nothing wife, no, if the price
   Were forty marks a spoonful,
   I'd give a thousand pound to purchase fruitfulness;
   'Tis but bating so many good works   145
   In the erecting of Bridewells and spital-houses,
   And so fetch it up again, for having none
   I mean to make good deeds my children.

LADY KIX
   Give me but those good deeds, and I'll find children.

SIR OLIVER
   Hang thee, thou hast had too many.   150

LADY KIX
   Thou li'st brevity.

---

132 *thirteen . . .* value of a mark, with a pun on the previous word
138–140 *cut . . . do withal* double entendre
145 *bating* diminishing
147 *fetch it up again* 'if I can't buy fruitfulness I'll save the money
    and be a philanthropist'

---

146 *Bridewells and spital-houses.* Bridewell, originally a royal palace, was
   given to London by Edward VI 'to be a house of correction for lewd
   and dissolute livers' (Speed, *The Theatre of . . . Great Britain* (1611),
   fol. 814); here used for prisons in general; spitals were hospitals,
   especially for leprosy and venereal disease.

SIR OLIVER

    O horrible, dar'st thou call me brevity?

    Dar'st thou be so short with me?

LADY KIX

    Thou deservest worse.

    Think but upon the goodly lands and livings   155

    That's kept back through want on't.

SIR OLIVER

    Talk not on't pray thee,

    Thou'lt make me play the woman and weep too.

LADY KIX

    'Tis our dry barrenness puffs up Sir Walter—

    None gets by your not-getting, but that knight;   160

    He's made by th'means, and fats his fortune shortly

    In a great dowry with a goldsmith's daughter.

SIR OLIVER

    They may all be deceived,

    Be but you patient wife.

LADY KIX

    I have suffered a long time.   165

SIR OLIVER

    Suffer thy heart out; a pox suffer thee!

LADY KIX

    Nay thee, thou desertless slave!

SIR OLIVER

    Come, come, I ha' done;

    You'll to the gossiping of Mr Allwit's child?

LADY KIX

    Yes, to my much joy;   170

    Everyone gets before me—there's my sister

    Was married but at Bartholomew eve last,

    And she can have two children at a birth;

    O one of them, one of them would ha' served my turn.

SIR OLIVER

    Sorrow consume thee, thou art still crossing me,   175

    And know'st my nature.

Enter a MAID

MAID   O mistress, weeping or railing,

    That's our house harmony.

169 *gossiping* christening

---

172 *Bartholomew eve.* 23 August; as it is now only Lent, the children arrived
    rather early in the marriage.

LADY KIX
  What sayst Jugg?
MAID
  The sweetest news.
LADY KIX
  What is't wench?   180
MAID
  Throw down your doctor's drugs,
  They're all but heretics; I bring certain remedy
  That has been taught, and proved, and never failed.
SIR OLIVER
  O that, that, that or nothing.
MAID
  There's a gentleman,   185
  I haply have his name, too, that has got
  Nine children by one water that he useth;
  It never misses, they come so fast upon him,
  He was fain to give it over.
LADY KIX   His name sweet Jugg?
MAID
  One Mr Touchwood, a fine gentleman,   190
  But run behind hand much with getting children.
SIR OLIVER
  Is't possible?
MAID   Why sir, he'll undertake
  Using that water, within fifteen year,
  For all your wealth, to make you a poor man,
  You shall so swarm with children.   195
SIR OLIVER
  I'll venture that i'faith.
LADY KIX   That shall you husband.
MAID
  But I must tell you first, he's very dear.
SIR OLIVER
  No matter, what serves wealth for?
LADY KIX   True sweet husband,
  There's land to come; put case his water stands me
  In some five hundred pound a pint,   200
  'Twill fetch a thousand, and a Kersten soul,
  And that's worth all sweet husband.
  I'll about it.   *Ex[eunt]*

186 *haply* by chance
199 *put case* suppose, with a pun on 'case' meaning vagina
201 *Kersten* Christian   202–203 Q reverses these two lines

[Act II, Scene ii]

Enter ALLWIT

ALLWIT

I'll go bid gossips presently myself,
That's all the work I'll do, nor need I stir,
But that it is my pleasure to walk forth
And air myself a little; I am tied to nothing
In this business, what I do is merely recreation, 5
Not constraint.
Here's running to and fro, nurse upon nurse,
Three charwomen, besides maids and neighbours' children.
Fie, what a trouble I have rid my hands on;
It makes me sweat to think on't.

Enter SIR WALTER WHOREHOUND

SIR WALTER How now Jack? 10

ALLWIT

I am going to bid gossips for your worship's child sir,
A goodly girl i'faith, give you joy on her,
She looks as if she had two thousand pound to her portion
And run away with a tailor; a fine plump black eyed slut,
Under correction sir, 15
I take delight to see her: Nurse!

Enter DRY NURSE

DRY NURSE Do you call sir?

ALLWIT

I call not you, I call the wet nurse hither, *Exit* [DRY NURSE]
Give me the wet nurse,

Enter WET NURSE [*carrying baby*]

ay, 'tis thou,
Come hither, come hither,
Let's see her once again; I cannot choose 20
But buss her thrice an hour.

WET NURSE

You may be proud on't sir,
'Tis the best piece of work that e'er you did.

1 *gossips* godparents here, but also women friends
16 s.d. (l.14 Q)   17 s.d. (l.16 Q)   18 s.d. (l.17 Q)
21 *buss* kiss

14 *tailor*. Tailors were traditionally lecherous; cf. Dekker and Webster,
Northward Ho!, 'Tailors will be saucy and lickerish' (II, i, 177).

ALLWIT
  Think'st thou so Nurse? What sayst to Wat and Nick?
WET NURSE
  They're pretty children both, but here's a wench   25
  Will be a knocker.
ALLWIT
  Pup—sayst thou me so? Pup, little countess;
  Faith sir I thank your worship for this girl,
  Ten thousand times, and upward.
SIR WALTER
  I am glad I have her for you sir.   30
ALLWIT
  Here, take her in Nurse, wipe her, and give her spoon-meat.
WET NURSE
  [*Aside*] Wipe your mouth sir.   *Exit*
ALLWIT
  And now about these gossips.
SIR WALTER
  Get but two, I'll stand for one myself.
ALLWIT
  To your own child sir?   35
SIR WALTER
  The better policy, it prevents suspicion,
  'Tis good to play with rumour at all weapons.
ALLWIT
  Troth, I commend your care sir, 'tis a thing
  That I should ne'er have thought on.
SIR WALTER   [*Aside*] The more slave;
  When man turns base, out goes his soul's pure flame,   40
  The fat of ease o'er-throws the eyes of shame.
ALLWIT
  I am studying who to get for godmother
  Suitable to your worship: now I ha' thought on't.
SIR WALTER
  I'll ease you of that care, and please myself in't.
  [*Aside*] My love the goldsmith's daughter, if I send,   45
  Her father will command her. Davy Dahumma!

                    Enter DAVY

26 *knocker* good-looker
31 *spoon-meat* puréed food for infants

32 *Wipe your mouth.* Make a fool of yourself (Bullen); may also refer to
   'Such is the way of an adulterous woman; she eateth, and wipeth her
   mouth, and saith, I have done no wickedness' (Proverbs XXX, 20).

ALLWIT

  I'll fit your worship then with a male partner.

SIR WALTER

  What is he?

ALLWIT

  A kind proper gentleman, brother to Mr Touchwood.

SIR WALTER

  I know Touchwood, has he a brother living?   50

ALLWIT

  A neat bachelor.

SIR WALTER

  Now we know him we'll make shift with him.

  Dispatch, the time draws near. Come hither Davy.

                        Exit [*with* DAVY]

ALLWIT

  In troth I pity him, he ne'er stands still.

  Poor knight, what pains he takes—sends this way one,   55

  That way another, has not an hour's leisure—

  I would not have thy toil, for all thy pleasure.

              Enter TWO PROMOTERS

  Ha, how now, what are these that stand so close

  At the street corner, pricking up their ears,

  And snuffing up their noses, like rich men's dogs   60

  When the first course goes in? By the mass, promoters,

  'Tis so I hold my life, and planted there

  To arrest the dead corps of poor calves and sheep,

  Like ravenous creditors that will not suffer

  The bodies of their poor departed debtors   65

  To go to th' grave, but e'en in death to vex

  And stay the corps, with bills of Middlesex.

  This Lent will fat the whoresons up with sweetbreads

  And lard their whores with lamb-stones; what their golls

  Can clutch goes presently to their Molls and Dolls.   70

  The bawds will be so fat with what they earn

---

51 *neat* elegant
63 *corps* corpses
69 *lamb-stones* lambs' testicles, believed to be aphrodisiac
69 *golls* hands (sl.)

---

67 *bills of Middlesex.* Writs allowing arrests on bogus charges within
    Middlesex, which contained London north of the Thames, so that
    defendants could be tried for crimes committed outside the county.

Their chins will hang like udders by Easter eve,
And being stroked, will give the milk of witches.
How did the mongrels hear my wife lies in?
Well, I may baffle 'em gallantly. By your favour gentlemen,   75
I am a stranger both unto the city
And to her carnal strictness.

1 PROMOTER   Good; your will sir?

ALLWIT
Pray tell me where one dwells that kills this Lent.

1 PROMOTER
How, kills? Come hither Dick,
A bird, a bird.   80

2 PROMOTER
What is't that you would have?

ALLWIT   · Faith any flesh,
But I long especially for veal and green sauce.

1 PROMOTER
[*Aside*] Green goose, you shall be sauced.

ALLWIT
I have half a scornful stomach, no fish will be admitted.

1 PROMOTER
Not this Lent sir?   85

ALLWIT
Lent, what cares colon here for Lent?

1 PROMOTER
You say well sir;
Good reason that the colon of a gentleman,
As you were lately pleased to term your worship sir,
Should be fulfilled with answerable food,   90
To sharpen blood, delight health, and tickle nature.
Were you directed hither to this street sir?

ALLWIT
That I was, ay marry.

75 *baffle* insult, treat with indignity
80 *bird* victim
83 *Green goose* young goose made into pies for the goose fair at Bow;
    also a cant term for a cuckold
86 *colon* largest intestine; Allwit would probably pat his stomach

---

72-73 *chins . . . witches.* Bawds were believed to be characterized by
    double chins; witches were believed to give suck to the devil, and their
    familiars, from a third nipple somewhere on the body. Middleton also
    uses this image in *The Black Book* (1604). (See Bullen, VIII (1886), 12.)
82 *green sauce.* Made with vinegar or verjuice with spices but without garlic;
    both 'veal' and 'green' imply gullibility.

2 PROMOTER
And the butcher belike
Should kill and sell close in some upper room? 95

ALLWIT
Some apple loft as I take it, or a coal house,
I know not which i'faith.

2 PROMOTER
Either will serve.
[*Aside*] This butcher shall kiss Newgate, 'less he turn up the
Bottom of the pocket of his apron; 100
You go to seek him?

ALLWIT Where you shall not find him;
I'll buy, walk by your noses with my flesh,
Sheep-biting mongrels, hand basket freebooters!
My wife lies in; a foutra for promoters! *Exit*

1 PROMOTER
That shall not serve your turn—what a rogue's this; how 105
cunningly he came over us!

Enter a MAN *with meat in a basket*

2 PROMOTER
Husht, stand close.

MAN
I have 'scaped well thus far; they say the knaves are
wondrous hot and busy.

1 PROMOTER
By your leave sir, 110
We must see what you have under your cloak there.

MAN
Have? I have nothing.

1 PROMOTER
No, do you tell us that? What makes this lump stick out
then; we must see sir.

MAN
What will you see sir—a pair of sheets, and two of my 115
wife's foul smocks, going to the washers?

2 PROMOTER
O we love that sight well, you cannot please us better:

99–100 *turn . . . apron* offer a bribe
103 *freebooters* pirates, here raiding the baskets of passers-by
104 *foutra* vulgarism for the sexual act; from the French 'foutre'
105 *serve your turn* continues the sense of 'foutra'

99 *Newgate.* One of the gates of ancient London, used as a prison from at
least the twelfth century until its demolition in 1777.

what, do you gull us? Call you these shirts and smocks?

MAN

  Now a pox choke you!

  You have cozened me and five of my wife's kindred   120

  Of a good dinner; we must make it up now

  With herrings and milk pottage.   *Exit*

1 PROMOTER

  'Tis all veal.

2 PROMOTER

  All veal? Pox the worse luck; I promised faithfully to send

  this morning a fat quarter of lamb to a kind gentlewoman in   125

  Turnbull street that longs, and how I'm crossed.

1 PROMOTER

  Let's share this, and see what hap comes next then.

Enter another with a basket

2 PROMOTER

  Agreed, stand close again; another booty.

  What's he?

1 PROMOTER

  Sir, by your favour.   130

MAN

  Meaning me sir?

1 PROMOTER

  Good Mr Oliver, cry thee mercy, i'faith.

  What has thou there?

MAN

  A rack of mutton sir, and half a lamb;

  You know my mistress's diet.   135

1 PROMOTER

  Go, go, we see thee not; away, keep close,

  Heart, let him pass, thou'lt never have the wit

  To know our benefactors.   [*Exit* MAN]

2 PROMOTER

  I have forgot him.

1 PROMOTER

  'Tis Mr Beggarland's man, the wealthy merchant   140

  That is in fee with us.

2 PROMOTER

  Now I have a feeling of him.

122 *milk pottage* milk broth
134 *rack* neck

---

126 *Turnbull street* ran between Clerkenwell Green and Cowcross street,
    and was the most notorious street in London for its thieves and whores.

1 PROMOTER
  You know he purchased the whole Lent together,
  Gave us ten groats apiece on Ash-Wednesday.
2 PROMOTER
  True, true.   145

Enter a WENCH *with a basket, and a child in it under a loin of*
                              mutton
1 PROMOTER
  A wench.
2 PROMOTER
  Why then stand close indeed.
WENCH
  [*Aside*] Women had need of wit, if they'll shift here,
  And she that hath wit may shift anywhere.
1 PROMOTER
  Look, look, poor fool,   150
  She has left the rump uncovered too,
  More to betray her; this is like a murderer
  That will outface the deed with a bloody band.
2 PROMOTER
  What time of the year is't sister?
WENCH
  O sweet gentlemen, I am a poor servant,   155
  Let me go.
1 PROMOTER
  You shall wench, but this must stay with us.
WENCH
  O you undo me sir;
  'Tis for a wealthy gentlewoman that takes physic sir,
  The doctor does allow my mistress mutton,   160
  O as you tender the dear life of a gentlewoman,
  I'll bring my master to you, he shall show you
  A true authority from the higher powers,
  And I'll run every foot.

144 *groats* first coined 1351–52, made equal to fourpence; by 1600
   used for any small sum
153 *band* collar; standing collars were popular 1605–30

---

143 'at the one time he bought protection for himself for the whole of Lent'.
s.d. The trick played by the country wench is also found in some ballads,
   e.g. 'The Country Girl's Policy, or the Cockney Outwitted' and 'A
   Tryall of Skill, performed by a poor decay'd Gentlewoman' (*Roxburghe
   Ballads*, ed. J. W. Ebsworth (1880–1890), VII, 286 and IX, 556).
163 *true authority*. The sick, and some foreign ambassadors, were permitted
   by the city authorities to have meat during Lent.

2 PROMOTER
      Well, leave your basket then,   165
      And run and spare not.
WENCH
      Will you swear then to me
      To keep it till I come.
1 PROMOTER
      Now by this light I will.
WENCH
      What say you gentleman?   170
2 PROMOTER
      What a strange wench 'tis.
      Would we might perish else.
WENCH
      Nay then I run sir.   *Exit*
1 PROMOTER
      And ne'er return I hope.
2 PROMOTER
      A politic baggage,   175
      She makes us swear to keep it;
      I prithee look what market she hath made.
1 PROMOTER
      Imprimis sir, a good fat loin of mutton;
      What comes next under this cloth?
      Now for a quarter of lamb.   180
2 PROMOTER
      Now for a shoulder of mutton.
1 PROMOTER
      Done.
2 PROMOTER
      Why done sir?
1 PROMOTER
      By the mass I feel I have lost,
      'Tis of more weight i'faith.   185
2 PROMOTER
      Some loin of veal?
1 PROMOTER
      No faith, here's a lamb's head,
      I feel that plainly, why yet I'll win my wager.

175 *politic* cunning
181 *Now* ed. (not Q)
188 *I'll* ed. (Q omits)

178 'In the first place'.

2 PROMOTER
  Ha?
1 PROMOTER
  Swounds what's here?   190
2 PROMOTER
  A child.
1 PROMOTER
  A pox of all dissembling cunning whores.
2 PROMOTER
  Here's an unlucky breakfast.
1 PROMOTER
  What shall's do?
2 PROMOTER
  The quean made us swear to keep it too.   195
1 PROMOTER
  We might leave it else.
2 PROMOTER
  Villainous strange;
  Life had she none to gull but poor promoters
  That watch hard for a living?
1 PROMOTER
  Half our gettings must run in sugar-sops   200
  And nurses' wages now, besides many a pound of soap,
  And tallow; we have need to get loins of mutton still,
  To save suet to change for candles.
2 PROMOTER
  Nothing mads me but this was a lamb's head with you, you
  felt it; she has made calves' heads of us.   205
1 PROMOTER
  Prithee no more on't,
  There's time to get it up; it is not come
  To mid-Lent Sunday yet.
2 PROMOTER
  I am so angry, I'll watch no more today.
1 PROMOTER
  Faith nor I neither.   210
2 PROMOTER
  Why then I'll make a motion.

---

200 *sugar-sops* bread soaked in sugar water
202 *tallow* for candles

204–205 *Nothing . . . us.* 'Nothing makes me so annoyed as to think that
  you, who felt the baby, said it was a lamb's head; she's made fools of us'.

1 PROMOTER
   Well, what is't?
2 PROMOTER
   Let's e'en go to the Checker at Queen-hive and roast the
   loin of mutton, till young flood; then send the child to
   Branford.   [*Exeunt*]   215

[Act II, Scene iii]

Enter ALLWIT *in one of Sir Walter's suits, and* DAVY *trussing him*

ALLWIT
   'Tis a busy day at our house Davy.
DAVY
   Always the kursning day sir.
ALLWIT
   Truss, truss me Davy.
DAVY
   [*Aside*] No matter and you were hanged sir.
ALLWIT
   How does this suit fit me Davy?   5
DAVY
   Excellent neatly; my master's things were ever fit for you
   sir, e'en to a hair you know.
ALLWIT
   Thou has hit it right Davy,
   We ever jumped in one, this ten years Davy.

                  Enter a SERVANT *with a box*

   So, well said; what art thou?   10

214 *young flood* the beginning of the rising tide
s.d. *trussing* tying the points of his hose to his doublet; 'to truss' also
     means 'to hang'
  2 *kursning day* christening day

213 *Checker.* An inn which gave its name to the lane where it stood (cf.
     Survey I, 231).
213 *Queen-hive.* Queenhithe, 'the very chief and principal water-gate of this
     city' (*Survey* I, 41), a quay on the north bank of the Thames.
215 *Branford.* Brentford, eight miles upstream from London and a resort
     of whores as well as other citizens; usually spelt 'Brainford', as at
     V, iv, 97.
  9 *jumped in one.* Agreed; but with a pun, of course; there are probably also
     puns on 'things', 'fit', and 'hair' ('heir') in the preceding speech.

SERVANT

Your comfit-maker's man sir.

ALLWIT

O sweet youth, into the nurse quick,
Quick, 'tis time i'faith;
Your mistress will be here?

SERVANT

She was setting forth sir.   15

Enter two PURITANS

ALLWIT

Here comes our gossips now, O I shall have such kissing
work today; sweet Mistress Underman welcome i'faith.

1 PURITAN

Give you joy of your fine girl sir,
Grant that her education may be pure,
And become one of the faithful.   20

ALLWIT

Thanks to your sisterly wishes Mistress Underman.

2 PURITAN

Are any of the brethren's wives yet come?

ALLWIT

There are some wives within, and some at home.

1 PURITAN

Verily thanks sir.   *Ex[eunt]*

ALLWIT

Verily you are an ass forsooth;   25
I must fit all these times, or there's no music.

Enter two GOSSIPS

Here comes a friendly and familiar pair,
Now I like these wenches well.

1 GOSSIP

How dost sirrah?

ALLWIT

Faith well I thank you neighbour, and how dost thou?   30

2 GOSSIP

Want nothing, but such getting sir as thine.

---

11 *comfit* sweet made by mixing the pulp of cooked fruit with sugar

26 'I have to be agreeable with all these people or else there'll be no
kissing'; cf. Dekker and Webster, *Westward Ho!* V, iv, 283–4, 'Every
husband play music upon the lips of his wife'. Allwit is out to enjoy
himself.

ALLWIT
  My gettings wench, they are poor.
1 GOSSIP
  Fie that thou'lt say so,
  Th'ast as fine children as a man can get.
DAVY
  [*Aside*] Ay, as a man can get,   35
  And that's my master.
ALLWIT
  They are pretty foolish things,
  Put to making in minutes;
  I ne'er stand long about 'em,
  Will you walk in wenches?   [*Exeunt* GOSSIPS]   40

        Enter TOUCHWOOD JUNIOR *and* MOLL

TOUCHWOOD JUNIOR
  The happiest meeting that our souls could wish for. Here's
  the ring ready; I am beholding unto your father's haste,
  h'as kept his hour.
MOLL
  He never kept it better.

        Enter SIR WALTER WHOREHOUND [*with goblet*]

TOUCHWOOD JUNIOR
  Back, be silent.   45
SIR WALTER
  Mistress and partner, I will put you both into one cup. [*Drinks*]
DAVY
  Into one cup, most proper,
  A fitting compliment for a goldsmith's daughter.
ALLWIT
  Yes sir, that's he must be your worship's partner
  In this day's business, Mr Touchwood's brother.   50
SIR WALTER
  I embrace your acquaintance sir.
TOUCHWOOD JUNIOR
  It vows your service sir.
SIR WALTER
  It's near high time, come Mr Allwit.
ALLWIT
  Ready sir.
SIR WALTER
  Will't please you walk?   55

  42 *beholding* beholden

TOUCHWOOD JUNIOR
Sir I obey your time. *Ex[eunt]*

Enter MIDWIFE *with the child,* [MAUDLIN] *and the* GOSSIPS *to the Kursning*

1 GOSSIP
Good Mrs Yellowhammer.

MAUDLIN
In faith I will not.

1 GOSSIP
Indeed it shall be yours.

MAUDLIN
I have sworn i'faith. 60

1 GOSSIP
I'll stand still then.

MAUDLIN
So will you let the child go without company
And make me forsworn.

1 GOSSIP
You are such another creature.

2 GOSSIP
Before me? I pray come down a little. 65

3 GOSSIP
Not a whit; I hope I know my place.

2 GOSSIP
Your place? Great wonder sure! Are you any better than a
comfit-maker's wife?

3 GOSSIP
And that's as good at all times as a 'pothecary's.

2 GOSSIP
Ye lie, yet I forbear you too. 70

1 PURITAN
Come sweet sister, we go in unity, and show the fruits of
peace like children of the spirit.

2 PURITAN
I love lowliness.

4 GOSSIP
True, so say I, though they strive more,
There comes as proud behind, as goes before. 75

5 GOSSIP
Every inch, i'faith. *Ex[eunt]*

---

s.d. During this progress across the stage, the women are squabbling over
precedence in following the child into the room.

75 *There comes as proud* ... Proverbial, but the meaning of 'proud' as
'sexually excited' is taken up in the next line.

Act III, [Scene i]

Enter TOUCHWOOD JUNIOR *and a* PARSON

TOUCHWOOD JUNIOR
O sir, if ever you felt the force of love, pity it in me.
PARSON
Yes, though I ne'er was married sir,
I have felt the force of love from good men's daughters,
And some that will be maids yet three years hence.
Have you got a licence? 5
TOUCHWOOD JUNIOR
Here 'tis ready sir.
PARSON
That's well.
TOUCHWOOD JUNIOR
The ring and all things perfect, she'll steal hither.
PARSON
She shall be welcome sir; I'll not be long
Aclapping you together. 10

Enter MOLL *and* TOUCHWOOD SENIOR

TOUCHWOOD JUNIOR
O here she's come sir.
PARSON
What's he?
TOUCHWOOD JUNIOR
My honest brother.
TOUCHWOOD SENIOR
Quick, make haste sirs.
MOLL
You must dispatch with all the speed you can, 15
For I shall be missed straight; I made hard shift
For this small time I have.
PARSON
Then I'll not linger,
Place that ring upon her finger,
This the finger plays the part, 20
Whose master vein shoots from the heart;
Now join hands.

5 *licence.* See note to II, i, 128.
21 *heart.* Popular superstition had it that a vein or nerve ran from the third finger of the left hand to the heart; cf. note to I, ii, 55–56.

Enter YELLOWHAMMER *and* SIR WALTER

YELLOWHAMMER
  Which I will sever,
  And so ne'er again meet never.
MOLL
  O we are betrayed.   25
TOUCHWOOD JUNIOR
  Hard fate.
SIR WALTER
  I am struck with wonder.
YELLOWHAMMER
  Was this the politic fetch, thou mystical baggage,
  Thou disobedient strumpet?
  And were you so wise to send for her to such an end?   30
SIR WALTER
  Now I disclaim the end, you'll make me mad.
YELLOWHAMMER
  And what are you sir?
TOUCHWOOD JUNIOR
  And you cannot see with those two glasses, put on a pair
  more.
YELLOWHAMMER
  I dreamt of anger still, here take your ring sir;   35
  Ha this? Life 'tis the same: abominable!
  Did not I sell this ring?
TOUCHWOOD JUNIOR
  I think you did, you received money for it.
YELLOWHAMMER
  Heart, hark you knight,
  Here's no inconscionable villainy—   40
  Set me awork to make the wedding ring,
  And come with an intent to steal my daughter;
  Did ever runaway match it?
SIR WALTER
  This your brother sir?
TOUCHWOOD SENIOR
  He can tell that as well as I.   45
YELLOWHAMMER
  The very posy mocks me to my face:
  Love that's wise, blinds parents' eyes.
  I thank your wisdom sir for blinding of us;

28 *fetch* trick, stratagem   30 *you* ed. (Q omits)
33 *And* if   33 *glasses* spectacles, or perhaps his eyes

We have good hope to recover our sight shortly,
In the meantime I will lock up this baggage,   50
As carefully as my gold; she shall see as little sun
If a close room or so can keep her from the light on't.

MOLL
O sweet father, for love's sake pity me.

YELLOWHAMMER
Away!

MOLL
Farewell sir, all content bless thee,   55
And take this for comfort,
Though violence keep me, thou canst lose me never,
I am ever thine although we part for ever.

YELLOWHAMMER
Ay we shall part you minx.
                            Exit [YELLOWHAMMER *with* MOLL]

SIR WALTER
Your acquaintance sir came very lately,   60
Yet it came too soon;
I must hereafter know you for no friend,
But one that I must shun like pestilence,
Or the disease of lust.

TOUCHWOOD JUNIOR
Like enough sir, you ha' ta'en me at the worst time for   65
words that e'er ye picked out; faith do not wrong me sir.
                                                    Exit

TOUCHWOOD SENIOR
Look after him and spare not; there he walks
That never yet received baffling; you're blessed
More than e'er I knew. Go take your rest.   *Exit*

SIR WALTER
I pardon you, you are both losers.   *Exit*   70

[Act III, Scene ii]

A bed thrust out upon the stage, ALLWIT'S WIFE *in it. Enter all the*
          GOSSIPS [*including* MAUDLIN *and* LADY KIX]

1 GOSSIP
How is't woman? We have brought you home
A kursen soul.

---

67 *Look . . . not.* Be continually wary of him   68 *baffling* insult

---

s.d. *A bed.* Cf. Heywood, *The Silver Age* III, i, 'Enter Semele drawn out in
her bed'.

MISTRESS ALLWIT
  Ay, I thank your pains.
1 PURITAN
  And verily well kursened, i'the right way,
  Without idolatry or superstition,   5
  After the pure manner of Amsterdam.
MISTRESS ALLWIT
  Sit down good neighbours; Nurse!
NURSE
  At hand forsooth.
MISTRESS ALLWIT
  Look they have all low stools.
NURSE
  They have forsooth.   10
2 GOSSIP
  Bring the child hither Nurse; how say you now
  Gossip, is't not a chopping girl, so like the father?
3 GOSSIP
  As if it had been spit out of his mouth,
  Eyed, nosed and browed as like a girl can be,
  Only indeed it has the mother's mouth.   15
2 GOSSIP
  The mother's mouth up and down, up and down.
3 GOSSIP
  'Tis a large child, she's but a little woman.
1 PURITAN
  No believe me, a very spiny creature, but all heart,
  Well mettled, like the faithful to endure
  Her tribulation here, and raise up seed.   20
2 GOSSIP
  She had a sore labour on't I warrant you, you can tell
  neighbour.
3 GOSSIP
  O she had great speed;
  We were afraid once,
  But she made us all have joyful hearts again;   25
  'Tis a good soul i'faith;
  The midwife found her a most cheerful daughter.

12 *chopping* vigorous, strapping
16 *up and down* exactly   18 *spiny* thin
19 *mettled* courageous, with a pun on the meaning 'amorous'

---

  6 *Amsterdam.* Meeting place and refuge for European dissenters, symbolic
  of Puritanism.

1 PURITAN
    'Tis the spirit, the sisters are all like her.

Enter SIR WALTER *with two spoons and plate and* ALLWIT

2 GOSSIP
    O here comes the chief gossip neighbours.

SIR WALTER
    The fatness of your wishes to you all ladies.   30

3 GOSSIP
    O dear sweet gentleman, what fine words he has—
    The fatness of our wishes.

2 GOSSIP
    Calls us all ladies.

4 GOSSIP
    I promise you a fine gentleman, and a courteous.

2 GOSSIP
    Methinks her husband shows like a clown to him.   35

3 GOSSIP
    I would not care what clown my husband were too, so I had
    such fine children.

2 GOSSIP
    She's all fine children gossip.

3 GOSSIP
    Ay, and see how fast they come.

1 PURITAN
    Children are blessings, if they be got with zeal,   40
    By the brethren, as I have five at home.

SIR WALTER
    The worst is past, I hope now gossip.

MISTRESS ALLWIT
    So I hope too good sir.

ALLWIT
    Why then so hope I too for company,
    I have nothing to do else.   45

SIR WALTER
    A poor remembrance lady,
    To the love of the babe; I pray accept of it.

MISTRESS ALLWIT
    O you are at too much charge sir.

2 GOSSIP
    Look, look, what has he given her, what is't gossip?

28 s.d. *plate* gold or silver ware
38 *She's* she has
40 *zeal* religious zeal, but also sexual enthusiasm (cf. I, i, 149)

3 GOSSIP

Now by my faith a fair high standing cup, and two great 50
postle spoons, one of them gilt.

1 PURITAN

Sure that was Judas then with the red beard.

2 PURITAN

I would not feed my daughter with that spoon for all the
world, for fear of colouring her hair; red hair the brethren
like not, it consumes them much, 'tis not the sisters' 55
colour.

Enter NURSE *with comfits and wine*

ALLWIT

Well said Nurse;
About, about with them amongst the gossips:
Now out comes all the tasseled handkerchers,
They are spread abroad between their knees already; 60
Now in goes the long fingers that are washed
Some thrice a day in urine—my wife uses it—
Now we shall have such pocketing;
See how they lurch at the lower end.

1 PURITAN

Come hither Nurse. 65

ALLWIT

Again! She has taken twice already.

1 PURITAN

I had forgot a sister's child that's sick.

ALLWIT

A pox, it seems your purity loves sweet things well that
puts in thrice together. Had this been all my cost now I had
been beggared. These women have no consciences at 70
sweetmeats, where e'er they come; see and they have not
culled out all the long plums too—they have left nothing here

50 *high standing cup* stemmed goblet
51 *postle spoons* usually silver, the handles ending in the figure of an
apostle, often given by sponsors at christenings
51 *gilt* silver covered with gold
55 *consumes* to burn, but also to consummate sexually
64 *lurch* filch, steal
72 *plums* sugar plums

---

52 *Judas . . . red beard.* Ancient belief; Judas wore a red beard in medieval
religious drama.
59 *tasseled.* Handkerchiefs were fashionably large, ornamental and had
tassels at the corners.
62 *urine* was used as a dentifrice as well as a cosmetic lotion.

but short riggle-tail comfits, not worth mouthing; no
mar'l I heard a citizen complain once that his wife's belly
only broke his back: mine had been all in fitters seven years   75
since, but for this worthy knight that with a prop upholds
my wife and me, and all my estate buried in Bucklersberrie.

MISTRESS ALLWIT
Here Mistress Yellowhammer, and neighbours,
To you all that have taken pains with me,   80
All the good wives at once.

1 PURITAN
I'll answer for them;
They wish all health and strength,
And that you may courageously go forward,
To perform the like and many such,   85
Like a true sister with motherly bearing.

ALLWIT
Now the cups troll about to wet the gossips' whistles;
It pours down i'faith: they never think of payment.

1 PURITAN
Fill again nurse.

ALLWIT
Now bless thee, two at once; I'll stay no longer;   90
It would kill me and if I paid for't.
Will it please you to walk down and leave the women?

SIR WALTER
With all my heart Jack.

ALLWIT
Troth I cannot blame you.

SIR WALTER
Sit you all merry ladies.   95

ALL GOSSIPS
Thank your worship sir.

1 PURITAN
Thank your worship sir.

---

73 *riggle-tail* tiny
75 *only* alone
75 *fitters* fragments   87 *troll* pass about

77–78 *Bucklersberrie* (Bucklersbury) ran south from the corner of Cheapside
    and the Poultry to Walbrook and 'on both the sides throughout is
    possessed of grocers and apothecaries' (*Survey* I, 260); Allwit is saying
    the catering for all the christenings of his wife's children over the years
    would have ruined him.

ALLWIT
A pox twice tipple ye, you are last and lowest.

Exit [ALLWIT *with* SIR WALTER]

1 PURITAN
Bring hither that same cup Nurse, I would fain drive
away this hup antichristian grief. [NURSE *refills goblet, then exit*] 100

3 GOSSIP
See gossip and she lies not in like a countess;
Would I had such a husband for my daughter.

4 GOSSIP
Is not she toward marriage?

3 GOSSIP
O no sweet gossip.

4 GOSSIP
Why, she's nineteen?   105

3 GOSSIP
Ay that she was last Lammas,
But she has a fault gossip, a secret fault.

4 GOSSIP
A fault, what is't?

3 GOSSIP
I'll tell you when I have drunk.

4 GOSSIP
Wine can do that, I see, that friendship cannot.   110

3 GOSSIP
And now I'll tell you gossip—she's too free.

4 GOSSIP
Too free?

3 GOSSIP
O ay, she cannot lie dry in her bed.

4 GOSSIP
What, and nineteen?

3 GOSSIP
'Tis as I tell you gossip.   115

[*Enter* NURSE *and speaks to* MAUDLIN]

 98 *tipple* tumble
106 *Lammas* 1 August; harvest festival of early English church

---

101 *countess*. The Countess of Salisbury 'lies in very richly, for the hanging
     of her chamber, being white satin, embroidered with gold (or silver) and
     pearl is valued at fourteen thousand pounds' (John Chamberlain,
     Letters, ed. N. E. McLure (Philadelphia, 1939), I, 415–416). This event
     took place at the end of January 1613.

MAUDLIN
  Speak with me Nurse? Who is't?
NURSE
  A gentleman from Cambridge,
  I think it be your son forsooth.
MAUDLIN
  'Tis my son Tim i'faith,
  Prithee call him up among the women,   [*Exit* NURSE]   120
  'Twill embolden him well,
  For he wants nothing but audacity;
  Would the Welsh gentlewoman at home were here now.
LADY KIX
  Is your son come forsooth?
MAUDLIN
  Yes from the university forsooth.   125
LADY KIX
  'Tis a great joy on ye.
MAUDLIN
  There's a great marriage towards for him.
LADY KIX
  A marriage?
MAUDLIN
  Yes sure, a huge heir in Wales,
  At least to nineteen mountains,   130
  Besides her goods and cattle.

                Enter TIM [*and* NURSE]

TIM
  O, I'm betrayed.   *Exit*
MAUDLIN
  What gone again? Run after him good Nurse; [*Exit* NURSE]
  He's so bashful, that's the spoil of youth;
  In the university they're kept still to men,   135
  And ne'er trained up to women's company.
LADY KIX
  'Tis a great spoil of youth indeed.

                Enter NURSE *and* TIM

NURSE
  Your mother will have it so.
MAUDLIN
  Why son, why Tim,
  What must I rise and fetch you? For shame son.   140

131 *cattle* property
135 *still* always

TIM

　Mother you do intreat like a freshwoman;
　'Tis against the laws of the university
　For any that has answered under bachelor
　To thrust 'mongst married wives.

MAUDLIN

　Come we'll excuse you here.   145

TIM

　Call up my tutor mother, and I care not.

MAUDLIN

　What is your tutor come, have you brought him up?

TIM

　I ha' not brought him up, he stands at door,
　Negatur, there's logic to begin with you mother.

MAUDLIN

　Run call the gentleman Nurse, he's my son's tutor;   150

　　　　　　　　　　　　　　　　　　[*Exit* NURSE]

　Here eat some plums.

TIM

　Come I from Cambridge, and offer me six plums?

MAUDLIN

　Why how now Tim,
　Will not your old tricks yet be left?

TIM

　Served like a child,   155
　When I have answered under bachelor?

MAUDLIN

　You'll never lin till I make your tutor whip you; you know
　how I served you once at the free school in Paul's church-
　yard?

TIM

　O monstrous absurdity!   160
　Ne'er was the like in Cambridge since my time;
　Life, whip a bachelor? You'd be laughed at soundly;
　Let not my tutor hear you,
　'Twould be a jest through the whole university;
　No more words mother.   165

---

141 *freshwoman* Tim's nonce word from 'freshman'　157 *lin* cease

157 *whip*. To be whipped as a disciplinary measure was a great disgrace.
158 *free school*. St. Paul's school was rebuilt and largely endowed in 1512 by
　　John Colet, Dean of Paul's, for 153 poor scholars; William Lily was the
　　first high master, but Tim may have been there under the illustrious
　　Richard Mulcaster (1596–1608)

Enter TUTOR

MAUDLIN
Is this your tutor Tim?

TUTOR
Yes surely lady, I am the man that brought him in league
with logic, and read the Dunces to him.

TIM
That did he mother, but now I have 'em all in my own
pate, and can as well read 'em to others.   170

TUTOR
That can he mistress, for they flow naturally from him.

MAUDLIN
I'm the more beholding to your pains sir.

TUTOR
Non ideo sane.

MAUDLIN
True, he was an idiot indeed
When he went out of London, but now he's well mended;   175
Did you receive the two goose pies I sent you?

TUTOR
And eat them heartily, thanks to your worship.

MAUDLIN
'Tis my son Tim, I pray bid him welcome gentlewomen.

TIM
Tim? Hark you Timotheus mother, Timotheus.

MAUDLIN
How, shall I deny your name? Timotheus quoth he?   180
Faith there's a name, 'tis my son Tim forsooth.

LADY KIX
You're welcome Mr Tim.   *Kiss*

TIM
O this is horrible, she wets as she kisses;
Your handkercher sweet tutor, to wipe them off, as fast
as they come on.   185

2 GOSSIP
Welcome from Cambridge.   *Kiss*

168 *Dunces*. Writings of Duns Scotus (1265?–1308?) and supporters of his
   theological views, which were attacked by the humanists and reformers
   of the 16th century.
173 'No indeed'.
176 *goose pies*. Made with a jointed goose, spices, ale, fried onions and wine,
   and baked in a paste; here the word accentuates Tim's foolishness.
182 s.d. *Kiss*. The English were at this time notorious for the freedom with
   which they kissed in greeting.

TIM

This is intolerable! This woman has a villainous sweet
breath, did she not stink of comfits; help me sweet tutor,
or I shall rub my lips off.

TUTOR

I'll go kiss the lower end the whilst.   190

TIM

Perhaps that's the sweeter, and we shall dispatch the sooner.

1 PURITAN

Let me come next. Welcome from the wellspring of
discipline, that waters all the brethren.   *Reels and falls*

TIM

Hoist I beseech thee.

3 GOSSIP

O bless the woman—Mistress Underman.   195

1 PURITAN

'Tis but the common affliction of the faithful,
We must embrace our falls.

TIM

I'm glad I 'scaped it, it was some rotten kiss sure,
It dropped down before it came at me.

Enter ALLWIT *and* DAVY

ALLWIT

Here's a noise, not parted yet?   200
Hyda, a looking glass; they have drunk so hard in plate,
That some of them had need of other vessels.
Yonder's the bravest show.

ALL GOSSIPS

Where? Where sir?

ALLWIT

Come along presently by the Pissing-conduit,   205
With two brave drums and a standard bearer.

200 *parted* departed
203 *show* procession

192–193 *Welcome . . . brethren.* Cambridge was the intellectual centre of
   Puritanism and its closeness to the Continent made it more accessible
   than Oxford to Calvinist influence.

201 *looking glass.* Chamber pot; but there may also be a pun: Mistress
   Underman is still on the floor and the sarcastic Allwit calls for a
   looking glass to see if she is still breathing; cf. *King Lear* V, iii, 262–5.

205 *Pissing-conduit.* Almost certainly the conduit at the western end of
   Cheapside, so named from the slenderness of its stream of water; the
   name was generic rather than specific.

ALL GOSSIPS

O brave.

TIM

Come tutor.   *Ex[eunt]*

ALL GOSSIPS

Farewell sweet gossip.   *Ex[eunt]*

MISTRESS ALLWIT

I thank you all for your pains.   210

1 PURITAN

Feed and grow strong.   *Exit*

ALLWIT

You had more need to sleep than eat;
Go take a nap with some of the brethren, go,
And rise up a well edified, boldified sister;
O here's a day of toil well passed o'er,   215
Able to make a citizen hare mad;
How hot they have made the room with their thick bums,
Dost not feel it Davy?

DAVY

Monstrous strong sir.

ALLWIT

What's here under the stools?   220

DAVY

Nothing but wet sir, some wine spilt here belike.

ALLWIT

Is't no worse thinkst thou?
Fair needlework stools cost nothing with them Davy.

DAVY

[*Aside*] Nor you neither i'faith.

ALLWIT

Look how they have laid them,   225
E'en as they lie themselves, with their heels up;
How they have shuffled up the rushes too Davy
With their short figging little shittle-cork heels;
These women can let nothing stand as they find it;

216 *hare mad*. Hares grow wilder in the breeding season, around March.
220 *stools*. Padded furniture was becoming fashionable, large sums being
    spent on embroidered coverings.
227 *rushes* indicate that rushes were strewn on the public theatre stage; cf.
    E. K. Chambers, *Elizabethan Stage* (1923), II, 529.
228 *figging*. A derisive term probably used here with bawdy overtones.
228 *shittle-cork*. Wedge heels (and soles) of cork were fashionable 1595–
    1620; 'shittle' = 'shuttle' as in 'shuttle-cock'.

But what's the secret thou'st about to tell me   230
My honest Davy?

DAVY

If you should disclose it sir—

ALLWIT

Life, rip my belly up to the throat then Davy.

DAVY

My master's upon marriage.

ALLWIT

Marriage Davy? Send me to hanging rather.   235

DAVY

[*Aside*] I have stung him.

ALLWIT

When, where, what is she Davy?

DAVY

E'en the same was gossip, and gave the spoon.

ALLWIT

I have no time to stay, nor scarce can speak,
I'll stop those wheels, or all the work will break.   *Exit* 240

DAVY

I knew 'twould prick. Thus do I fashion still
All mine own ends by him and his rank toil;
'Tis my desire to keep him still from marriage;
Being his poor nearest kinsman, I may fare
The better at his death, there my hopes build   245
Since my Lady Kix is dry, and hath no child.   *Exit*

[Act III, Scene iii]

Enter both the TOUCHWOODS

TOUCHWOOD JUNIOR

Y'are in the happiest way to enrich yourself,
And pleasure me brother, as man's feet can tread in,
For though she be locked up, her vow is fixed only to me;
Then time shall never grieve me, for by that vow,
E'en absent I enjoy her, assuredly confirmed that none   5
Else shall, which will make tedious years seem gameful
To me. In the mean space lose you no time sweet brother;

5 I ed. (Q omits)
6 *gameful* joyful

239–240 *speak . . . break.* A common rhyme; cf. Thomas Morley's lyric,
'Now is the month of Maying' ('ea' = 'a' sound in 'bake').

You have the means to strike at this knight's fortunes
And lay him level with his bankrupt merit;
Get but his wife with child, perch at tree top,   10
And shake the golden fruit into her lap.
About it before she weep herself to a dry ground,
And whine out all her goodness.

TOUCHWOOD SENIOR

Prithee cease, I find a too much aptness in my blood
For such a business without provocation;   15
You might'well spared this banquet of eringoes,
Artichokes, potatoes, and your buttered crab,
They were fitter kept for your own wedding dinner.

TOUCHWOOD JUNIOR

Nay and you'll follow my suit, and save my purse too,
Fortune dotes on me; he's in happy case   20
Finds such an honest friend i'the common place.

TOUCHWOOD SENIOR

Life what makes thee so merry? Thou hast no cause
That I could hear of lately since thy crosses,
Unless there be news come, with new additions.

TOUCHWOOD JUNIOR

Why there thou hast it right,   25
I look for her this evening brother.

TOUCHWOOD SENIOR

How's that, look for her?

TOUCHWOOD JUNIOR

I will deliver you of the wonder straight brother:
By the firm secrecy and kind assistance
Of a good wench i'the house, who, made of pity,   30
Weighing the case her own, she's led through gutters,
Strange hidden ways, which none but love could find,
Or ha'the heart to venture; I expect her
Where you would little think.

TOUCHWOOD SENIOR

I care not where, so she be safe, and yours.   35

TOUCHWOOD JUNIOR

Hope tells me so,
But from your love and time my peace must grow.   *Exit*

16 *might'well spared* might as well have spared
21 *common place* court of common pleas at Westminster

16–17 *eringoes . . . crab.* All thought to be aphrodisiacs; 'eringo' was the
candied fruit of sea holly, 'potato' was probably the sweet potato or
yam; cf. John Marston, *The Scourge of Villainy*, Satire III, ll. 67–74.

TOUCHWOOD SENIOR
　You know the worst then brother; now to my Kix,
　The barren he and she, they're i'the next room,
　But to say which of their two humours hold them　　　　40
　Now at this instant, I cannot say truly.

SIR OLIVER
　Thou liest barrenness.　　　　KIX *to his* LADY *within*

TOUCHWOOD SENIOR
　O is't that time of day? Give you joy of your tongue,
　There's nothing else good in you; this their life
　The whole day from eyes open to eyes shut,　　　　45
　Kissing or scolding, and then must be made friends,
　Then rail the second part of the first fit out,
　And then be pleased again, no man knows which way,
　Fall out like giants, and fall in like children—
　Their fruit can witness as much.　　　　50

　　　　Enter SIR OLIVER KIX *and his* LADY

SIR OLIVER
　'Tis thy fault.

LADY KIX
　Mine, drouth and coldness?

SIR OLIVER
　Thine, 'tis thou art barren.

LADY KIX
　I barren! O life that I durst but speak now,
　In mine own justice, in mine own right—I barren!　　　　55
　'Twas otherways with me when I was at court,
　I was ne'er called so till I was married.

SIR OLIVER
　I'll be divorced.

LADY KIX　　　　Be hanged! I need not wish it,
　That will come too soon to thee:
　I may say, marriage and hanging goes by destiny,　　　　60
　For all the goodness I can find in't yet.

40 *humours* moods, dispositions
47 *fit* section of song or poem
52 *drouth* drought

56 *court.* Another reference to loose living in high places; cf. V. C. Gilder-
　sleeve, *Government Regulations of Elizabethan Drama* (1908), p. 109.
58 *divorced.* Sir Oliver would have found it difficult, as legislation was
　necessary for divorce; ecclesiastical courts could grant a separation for
　adultery or cruelty or annulment for an illegally contracted marriage but
　remarriage was forbidden.

SIR OLIVER
  I'll give up house, and keep some fruitful whore,
  Like an old bachelor in a tradesman's chamber;
  She and her children shall have all.
LADY KIX
  Where be they?   65
TOUCHWOOD SENIOR
  Pray cease;
  When there are friendlier courses took for you
  To get and multiply within your house,
  At your own proper costs in spite of censure,
  Methinks an honest peace might be established.   70
SIR OLIVER
  What with her? Never.
TOUCHWOOD SENIOR
  Sweet sir.
SIR OLIVER
  You work all in vain.
LADY KIX
  Then he doth all like thee.
TOUCHWOOD SENIOR
  Let me intreat sir.   75
SIR OLIVER
  Singleness confound her,
  I took her with one smock.
LADY KIX
  But indeed you came not so single,
  When you came from shipboard.
SIR OLIVER
  Heart she bit sore there;   80
  Prithee make's friends.
TOUCHWOOD SENIOR
  Is't come to that? The peal begins to cease.
SIR OLIVER
  I'll sell all at an outcry.
LADY KIX
  Do thy worst slave;
  Good sweet sir bring us into love again.   85

77 *one smock* i.e., very little property
83 *outcry* auction, proclaimed by the common crier

---

78 *single*. Celibate; but Wall remarks, probably on the basis of Sir Oliver's
    reply, 'Perhaps Lady Kix is suggesting that Sir Oliver came ashore
    lice-ridden'.

TOUCHWOOD SENIOR
  Some would think this impossible to compass;
  Pray let this storm fly over.
SIR OLIVER
  Good sir pardon me, I'm master of this house,
  Which I'll sell presently, I'll clap up bills this evening.
TOUCHWOOD SENIOR
  Lady, friends—come?   90
LADY KIX
  If e'er ye loved woman, talk not on't sir;
  What, friends with him? Good faith do you think I'm mad?
  With one that's scarce the hinder quarter of a man?
SIR OLIVER
  Thou art nothing of a woman.
LADY KIX
  Would I were less than nothing.   *Weeps*   95
SIR OLIVER
  Nay prithee what dost mean?
LADY KIX
  I cannot please you.
SIR OLIVER
  I'faith thou art a good soul, he lies that says it;
  Buss, buss, pretty rogue.
LADY KIX
  You care not for me.   100
TOUCHWOOD SENIOR
  Can any man tell now which way they came in?
  By this light I'll be hanged then.
SIR OLIVER
  Is the drink come?
TOUCHWOOD SENIOR
  Here's a little vial of almond-milk   *Aside*
  That stood me in some three pence.   105
SIR OLIVER
  I hope to see thee wench within these few years,
  Circled with children, pranking up a girl,
  And putting jewels in their little ears;
  Fine sport i'faith.

  89 *presently* at once   107 *pranking up* dressing smartly

  ---

  104 *almond-milk*. Made from sweet almonds, pounded, with water, stirred
      into thick barley water, sweetened and boiled; used in milk puddings.
  108 *their*. Dyce and Bullen emend to 'her', but both sexes wore earrings
      until about 1660.

LADY KIX

    Ay had you been aught, husband,   110

    It had been done ere this time.

SIR OLIVER

    Had I been aught, hang thee, hadst thou been aught;

    But a cross thing I ever found thee.

LADY KIX

    Thou art a grub to say so.

SIR OLIVER

    A pox on thee.   115

TOUCHWOOD SENIOR

    By this light they are out again at the same door,

    And no man can tell which way;

    Come here's your drink sir.

SIR OLIVER

    I will not take it now sir,

    And I were sure to get three boys ere midnight.   120

LADY KIX

    Why there thou show'st now of what breed thou com'st;

    To hinder generation! O thou villain,

    That knows how crookedly the world goes with us

    For want of heirs, yet put by all good fortune.

SIR OLIVER

    Hang strumpet, I will take it now in spite.   **125**

TOUCHWOOD SENIOR

    Then you must ride upon't five hours.

SIR OLIVER

    I mean so. Within there?

Enter a SERVANT

SERVANT

    Sir?

SIR OLIVER

    Saddle the white mare,   [*Exit* SERVANT]

    I'll take a whore along, and ride to Ware.   130

LADY KIX

    Ride to the devil.

SIR OLIVER

    I'll plague you every way;

    Look ye, do you see, 'tis gone.   *Drinks*

110 *aught* anything

---

130 *Ware.* 20 miles north of London, like Brentford a trysting place for
lovers legal and illicit; the Saracen's Head inn contained the Great Bed
of Ware, 10 ft 9 in square, now in the Victoria and Albert Museum.

LADY KIX
  A pox go with it.
SIR OLIVER
  I curse and spare not now.   135
TOUCHWOOD SENIOR
  Stir up and down sir, you must not stand.
SIR OLIVER
  Nay I'm not given to standing.
TOUCHWOOD SENIOR
  So much the better sir for the—
SIR OLIVER
  I never could stand long in one place yet,
  I learnt it of my father, ever figient;   140
  How if I crossed this sir?   *Capers*
TOUCHWOOD SENIOR
  O passing good sir, and would show well ahorseback; when
  you come to your inn, if you leapt over a joint-stool or two
  'twere not amiss, although you brake your neck sir.   *Aside*
SIR OLIVER
  What say you to a table thus high sir?   145
TOUCHWOOD SENIOR
  Nothing better sir, if it be furnished with good victuals.
  You remember how the bargain runs about this business?
SIR OLIVER
  Or else I had a bad head: you must receive sir four hundred
  pounds of me at four several payments: one hundred pound
  now in hand.   150
TOUCHWOOD SENIOR
  Right, that I have sir.
SIR OLIVER
  Another hundred when my wife is quick: the third when
  she's brought to bed: and the last hundred when the child
  cries; for if it should be stillborn, it doth no good sir.

140 *figient* restless, fidgety
141 *crossed* jumped across [a table or chair] (Dyce)
143 *joint-stool* solidly constructed of pieces fitted together, often
    carved, about 2 ft. high; very common
148 *bad head* ironic reference to cuckold's horns
152 *wife* ed. (wifes Q)

138 The lacuna here and elsewhere in the play may indicate that the actor
    is to *ad lib*, or whisper to his listener; alternatively, that the censor may
    have deleted something.

TOUCHWOOD SENIOR
  All this is even still; a little faster sir.   155
SIR OLIVER
  Not a whit sir,
  I'm in an excellent pace for any physic.

Enter a SERVANT

SERVANT
  Your white mare's ready.
SIR OLIVER
  I shall up presently: one kiss, and farewell.
LADY KIX
  Thou shalt have two love.   160
SIR OLIVER
  Expect me about three.   *Exit [with* SERVANT]
LADY KIX
  With all my heart sweet.
TOUCHWOOD SENIOR
  By this light they have forgot their anger since,
  And are as far in again as e'er they were;
  Which way the devil came they? Heart I saw 'em not,   165
  Their ways are beyond finding out. Come sweet lady.
LADY KIX
  How must I take mine sir?
TOUCHWOOD SENIOR
  Clean contrary, yours must be taken lying.
LADY KIX
  Abed sir?
TOUCHWOOD SENIOR
  Abed, or where you will for your own ease;   170
  Your coach will serve.
LADY KIX   The physic must needs please.
                                   Ex[eunt]

155 *faster.* Sir Oliver has been capering all this while.
171 *coach.* First introduced in 1564, coaches were popular by the early 17th
     century and Dekker remarks, 'close caroaches were made running
     bawdy-houses' (*The Owl's Almanac* (1618), p. 8); a pun on 'coach' =
     'tutor' (and 'serve' in the sexual sense) is possible, though *O.E.D.* cites
     1848 as earliest date for such usage.

Act IV, [Scene i]

Enter TIM *and* TUTOR

TIM
Negatur argumentum tutor.

TUTOR
Probo tibi pupil, *stultus non est animal rationale.*

TIM
Falleris sane.

TUTOR
Quæso ut taceas, probo tibi.

TIM
Quomodo probas domine?   5

TUTOR
Stultus non habet rationem, ergo non est animal rationale.

TIM
*Sic argumentaris domine, stultus non habet rationem, ergo
non est animal rationale, negatur argumentum* again tutor.

TUTOR
*Argumentum iterum probo tibi domine, qui non participat de
ratione nullo modo potest vocari rationalibus,* but *stultus non*   10
*participat de ratione, ergo stultus nullo modo potest dicere
rationalis.*

TIM
Participat.

TUTOR
Sic disputus, qui participat quomodo participat.

TIM
Ut homo, probabo tibi in syllogismo.   15

11 *de (ac* Folger Q)

1–18 *Tim.* Your argument is denied, tutor. *Tut.* I am proving to you,
pupil, that a fool is not a rational animal. *Tim.* Indeed you will be wrong.
Tut. I ask you to be silent, I am showing you. *Tim.* How will you prove
it, master? *Tut.* A fool has no reason, therefore he is not a rational
animal. *Tim.* Thus you argue, master, a fool does not have reason,
therefore he is not a reasonable animal; your argument is denied again,
tutor. *Tut.* I will demonstrate the argument to you again, sir: he who
doesn't partake of reason can in no way be called rational, but a fool
does not partake of reason, therefore a fool can in no way be called
rational. *Tim.* He does partake. *Tut.* So you hold; how does the partaker
partake? *Tim.* As a man; I will prove it to you in a syllogism. *Tut.* Prove
it. *Tim.* I prove it thus, master: a fool is a man just as you and I are, man
is a rational animal, just as a fool is a rational animal.

TUTOR
Hunc proba.

TIM
*Sic probo domine, stultus est homo sicut tu et ego sum, homo
est animal rationale, sicut stultus est animal rationale.*

Enter MAUDLIN

MAUDLIN
Here's nothing but disputing all the day long with 'em.

TUTOR
Sic disputus, stultus est homo sicut tu et ego sum homo est   20
animal rationale, sicut stultus est animal rationale.

MAUDLIN
Your reasons are both good what e'er they be;
Pray give them o'er, faith you'll tire yourselves,
What's the matter between you?

TIM
Nothing but reasoning about a fool, mother.   25

MAUDLIN
About a fool, son? Alas what need you trouble your heads
about that, none of us all but knows what a fool is.

TIM
Why what's a fool, mother?
I come to you now.

MAUDLIN
Why one that's married before he has wit.   30

TIM
'Tis pretty i'faith, and well guessed of a woman never
brought up at the university: but bring forth what fool you
will mother, I'll prove him to be as reasonable a creature, as
myself or my tutor here.

MAUDLIN
Fie 'tis impossible.   35

TUTOR
Nay he shall do't forsooth.

TIM
'Tis the easiest thing to prove a fool by logic,
By logic I'll prove anything.

MAUDLIN
What thou wilt not?

TIM
I'll prove a whore to be an honest woman.   40

20–21 *Tut.* So you contend: a fool is a man just as you and I are, man is a
   rational animal, just as a fool is a rational animal.

MAUDLIN

Nay by my faith, she must prove that herself, or logic will
never do't.

TIM

'Twill do't I tell you.

MAUDLIN

Some in this street would give a thousand pounds that you
could prove their wives so.   45

TIM

Faith I can, and all their daughters too, though they had
three bastards. When comes your tailor hither?

MAUDLIN

Why what of him?

TIM

By logic I'll prove him to be a man,
Let him come when he will.   50

MAUDLIN

How hard at first was learning to him? Truly sir I thought
he would never a took the Latin tongue. How many
Accidences do you think he wore out ere he came to his
Grammar?

TUTOR

Some three or four.   55

MAUDLIN

Believe me sir, some four and thirty.

TIM

Pish I made haberdines of 'em in church porches.

MAUDLIN

He was eight years in his Grammar, and stuck horribly at a
foolish place there called *as in presenti*.

TIM

Pox I have it here now.   60

---

47 *tailor*. Tailors, especially women's, were considered unmanly; cf.
   nursery rhyme, 'Four and twenty tailors/Went to kill a snail'.
53 *Accidences*. Books of Latin grammar; Tim was, not surprisingly, a slow
   learner it seems.
57 *haberdines*. Salt dried codfish; Dyce suggests, 'Perhaps Tim alludes to
   some childish sport'. As 'cod' means 'scrotum', however, this is probably the first of a series of *doubles entendres* concluded when Maudlin
   invites the tutor to 'withdraw a little into my husband's chamber'.
59 *as in presenti*. Introductory phrase in the part of Lily and Colet's *A
   Short Introduction to Grammar* (1549) dealing with inflections of verbs;
   several writers make puns on it, e.g. Marston, *What You Will*, II, i.

MAUDLIN
>He so shamed me once before an honest gentleman that
>knew me when I was a maid.

TIM
>These women must have all out.

MAUDLIN
>*Quid est grammatica?* Says the gentleman to him (I shall
>remember by a sweet, sweet token) but nothing could he   65
>answer.

TUTOR
>How now pupil, ha, *quid est grammatica?*

TIM
>*Grammatica?* Ha, ha, ha.

MAUDLIN
>Nay do not laugh son, but let me hear you say it now: there
>was one word went so prettily off the gentleman's tongue, I   70
>shall remember it the longest day of my life.

TUTOR
>Come, *quid est grammatica?*

TIM
>Are you not ashamed tutor, *grammatica?* Why, *recte scribendi*
>*atque loquendi ars*, sir-reverence of my mother.

MAUDLIN
>That was it i'faith: why now son I see you are a deep   75
>scholar; and master tutor a word I pray, let us withdraw a
>little into my husband's chamber; I'll send in the North
>Wales gentlewoman to him, she looks for wooing: I'll
>put together both, and lock the door.

TUTOR
>I give great approbation to your conclusion.   80
>>   *Exit [with* MAUDLIN]

TIM
>I mar'l what this gentlewoman should be
>That I should have in marriage, she's a stranger to me:
>I wonder what my parents mean i'faith,
>To match me with a stranger so:
>A maid that's neither kiff nor kin to me: 85

85 *kiff* kith

---

64 'What is grammar?'

73–74 'The art of speaking and writing correctly'; (see J. D. Reeves,
   'Middleton and Lily's Grammar', *N & Q*, CXCVII (1952), 75–76).

74 *sir-reverence.* (i) with apologies to; (ii) excrement (continuing the pun
   on *ars*).

Life do they think I have no more care of my body,
Than to lie with one that I ne'er knew,
A mere stranger,
One that ne'er went to school with me neither,
Nor ever playfellows together?   90
They're mightily o'erseen in't methinks;
They say she has mountains to her marriage,
She's full of cattle, some two thousand runts;
Now what the meaning of these runts should be,
My tutor cannot tell me;   95
I have looked in Rider's dictionary for the letter R,
And there I can hear no tidings of these runts neither;
Unless they should be Rumford hogs,
I know them not,

                    Enter WELSH GENTLEWOMAN

And here she comes.   100
If I know what to say to her now
In the way of marriage, I'm no graduate;
Methinks i'faith 'tis boldly done of her
To come into my chamber being but a stranger;
She shall not say I'm so proud yet, but I'll speak to her: 105
Marry as I will order it,
She shall take no hold of my words I'll warrant her;
She looks and makes a curtsey—
Salve tu quoque puella pulcherrima,
Quid vis nescio nec sane curo—   110
Tully's own phrase to a heart.
WELSH GENTLEWOMAN
I know not what he means;
A suitor quotha?
I hold my life he understands no English.

91 *o'erseen* mistaken
93 *runts* small breed of Welsh and Highland cattle
111 *Tully's* Cicero's

---

96 *Rider's dictionary.* English-Latin and Latin-English dictionary com-
  piled by the Bishop of Killaloe, John Rider, first published at Oxford
  in 1589.
98 *Rumford* (Romford) in Essex 12 miles north-east of London, held hog
  markets on Tuesdays and grain and cattle markets on Wednesdays.
109–110 'Hail to you too, most beautiful maiden; what you want I don't
  know and I certainly don't care'.

TIM

Fertur me hercule tu virgo,   115
Wallia ut opibus abundis maximis.

WELSH GENTLEWOMAN

What's this *fertur* and *abundundis*?
He mocks me sure, and calls me a bundle of farts.

TIM

I have no Latin word now for their runts; I'll make some
shift or other: *Iterum dico opibus abundat maximis montibus*   120
et fontibus et ut ita dicam rontibus, attamen vero homanculus
ego sum natura simule arte bachalarius lecto profecto non
parata.

WELSH GENTLEWOMAN

This is most strange; may be he can speak Welsh—
Avedera whee comrage, derdue cog foginis?   125

TIM

Cog foggin? I scorn to cog with her, I'll tell her so too, in a
word near her own language: *Ego non cogo.*

WELSH GENTLEWOMAN

Rhegosin a whiggin harle ron corid ambre.

TIM

By my faith she's a good scholar, I see that already;
She has the tongues plain, I hold my life she has travelled;   130
What will folks say? There goes the learned couple;
Faith if the truth were known, she hath proceeded.

Enter MAUDLIN

MAUDLIN

How now, how speeds your business?

TIM

I'm glad my mother's come to part us.

132 *proceeded* taken a higher degree (cf. I, i, 154)

115–116 'It's said, by Hercules, young lady, that Wales has the greatest
     abundance of riches'.
120–123 'Again I say that you abound in resources, in the greatest mountains
     and fountains and, as I could say, runts; however I am truly but a little
     chap by nature and by art a bachelor, not actually ready for bed.' The
     Latin is by no means clear.
125 'Can you speak Welsh, for God's sake are you pretending with me?' A
     phonetic rendering for '*A fedrwch chwi Cymraeg, er Duw cog fo gennyf?*'
     (The final 's' may be due to a misreading of the copytext.)
126 *Cog.* Probably a pun on 'cog' = 'lie' ('deceive').
127 'I won't come together [with you]'.
128 Apparently undecipherable; the first part could mean 'Bring cheese and
     whey', a phonetic rendering of '*Dyre gosyn a chwig(gin?)*'.

MAUDLIN
How do you agree forsooth?   135
WELSH GENTLEWOMAN
As well as e'er we did before we met.
MAUDLIN
How's that?
WELSH GENTLEWOMAN
You put me to a man I understand not;
Your son's no English man methinks.
MAUDLIN
No English man, bless my boy,   140
And born i'the heart of London?
WELSH GENTLEWOMAN
I ha' been long enough in the chamber with him,
And I find neither Welsh nor English in him.
MAUDLIN
Why Tim, how have you used the gentlewoman?
TIM
As well as a man might do, mother, in modest Latin. 145
MAUDLIN
Latin, fool?
TIM
And she recoiled in Hebrew.
MAUDLIN
In Hebrew, fool? 'Tis Welsh.
TIM
All comes to one, mother.
MAUDLIN
She can speak English too.   150
TIM
Who told me so much?
Heart, and she can speak English, I'll clap to her,
I thought you'd marry me to a stranger.
MAUDLIN
You must forgive him, he's so inured to Latin,
He and his tutor, that he hath quite forgot   155
To use the Protestant tongue.
WELSH GENTLEWOMAN
'Tis quickly pardoned forsooth.
MAUDLIN
Tim make amends and kiss her,
He makes towards you forsooth.

147 *recoiled* answered

TIM

    O delicious, one may discover her country by her kissing.   160
    'Tis a true saying, there's nothing tastes so sweet as your
    Welsh mutton: it was reported you could sing.

MAUDLIN

    O rarely Tim, the sweetest British songs.

TIM

    And 'tis my mind, I swear, before I marry
    I would see all my wife's good parts at once,   165
    To view how rich I were.

MAUDLIN

    Thou shalt hear sweet music Tim.
    Pray, forsooth.   *Music and Welsh song*

THE SONG

[WELSH GENTLEWOMAN]

        Cupid is Venus' only joy,
        But he is a wanton boy,   170
        A very, very wanton boy,
        He shoots at ladies' naked breasts,
        He is the cause of most men's crests,
        I mean upon the forehead,
        Invisible but horrid;   175
        'Twas he first taught upon the way
        To keep a lady's lips in play.

        Why should not Venus chide her son,
        For the pranks that he hath done,
        The wanton pranks that he hath done?   180
        He shoots his fiery darts so thick,
        They hurt poor ladies to the quick,
        Ah me, with cruel wounding;
        His darts are so confounding,
        That life and sense would soon decay,   185
        But that he keeps their lips in play.

160 *country* a familiar pun (cf. *Hamlet*, III, ii, 120–1)
162 *sing* used again with a sexual sense; cf. II, i, 52
173 *crests* cuckolds' horns

---

162 *Welsh mutton* was famous, but Tim's speech is all *double entendre* of
    course.
169–194 'The first nine lines of this song, with two additional lines, occur in
    More Dissemblers besides Women, Act i, Scene 4' (Bullen).

Can there be any part of bliss,
In a quickly fleeting kiss,
A quickly fleeting kiss?
To one's pleasure, leisures are but waste,   190
The slowest kiss makes too much haste,
And lose it ere we find it,
The pleasing sport they only know,
That close above and close below.

TIM
I would not change my wife for a kingdom;   195
I can do somewhat too in my own lodging.

Enter YELLOWHAMMER *and* ALLWIT

YELLOWHAMMER
Why well said Tim, the bells go merrily,
I love such peals alife; wife lead them in a while,
Here's a strange gentleman desires private conference.
          [*Exeunt* MAUDLIN, TIM *and* WELSH GENTLEWOMAN]
You're welcome sir, the more for your name's sake.   200
Good Master Yellowhammer, I love my name well,
And which o'the Yellowhammers take you descent from,
If I may be so bold with you, which, I pray?

ALLWIT
The Yellowhammers in Oxfordshire,
Near Abbington.   205

YELLOWHAMMER
And those are the best Yellowhammers, and truest bred: I
came from thence myself, though now a citizen: I'll be
bold with you: you are most welcome.

ALLWIT
I hope the zeal I bring with me shall deserve it.

YELLOWHAMMER
I hope no less; what is your will sir?   210

ALLWIT
I understand by rumours, you have a daughter,
Which my bold love shall henceforth title cousin.

YELLOWHAMMER
I thank you for her sir.

---

198 *alife* as my life; extremely

196 *lodging.* On my own account; Bullen unnecessarily adds s.d. *Sings.*
205 *Abbington* (Abingdon), 56 miles north-west of London; about five miles
    south of Oxford.

ALLWIT

I heard of her virtues, and other confirmed graces.

YELLOWHAMMER

A plaguy girl sir. 215

ALLWIT

Fame sets her out with richer ornaments
Than you are pleased to boast of; 'tis done modestly;
I hear she's towards marriage.

YELLOWHAMMER

You hear truth sir.

ALLWIT

And with a knight in town, Sir Walter Whorehound. 220

YELLOWHAMMER

The very same sir.

ALLWIT

I am the sorrier for't.

YELLOWHAMMER

The sorrier? Why cousin?

ALLWIT

'Tis not too far past is't? It may be yet recalled?

YELLOWHAMMER

Recalled, why good sir? 225

ALLWIT

Resolve me in that point, ye shall hear from me.

YELLOWHAMMER

There's no contract passed.

ALLWIT

I am very joyful sir.

YELLOWHAMMER

But he's the man must bed her.

ALLWIT

By no means coz, she's quite undone then, 230
And you'll curse the time that e'er you made the match;
He's an arrant whoremaster, consumes his time and state,
——whom in my knowledge he hath kept this seven years,
Nay coz, another man's wife too.

---

226 *Resolve . . . point* satisfy me   227 *passed* (past Q)

---

227 *contract.* A *de praesenti* contract of marriage was made by two people
agreeing to take each other as man and wife, before witnesses, and was held
to be binding (cf. Webster, *The Duchess of Malfi*, II, i, 392); a contract *de
futuro* was an agreement to marry in the future and could be broken.

233 The lacunae here and four lines further on are in Q; see note to III, iii,
138.

YELLOWHAMMER
O abominable!   235
ALLWIT
Maintains the whole house, apparels the husband,
Pays servants' wages, not so much, but——
YELLOWHAMMER
Worse and worse, and doth the husband know this?
ALLWIT
Knows? Ay and glad he may too, 'tis his living;
As other trades thrive, butchers by selling flesh,   240
Poulters by venting conies, or the like coz.
YELLOWHAMMER
What an incomparable wittol's this?
ALLWIT
Tush, what cares he for that?
Believe me coz, no more than I do.
YELLOWHAMMER
What a base slave is that?   245
ALLWIT
All's one to him; he feeds and takes his ease,
Was ne'er the man that ever broke his sleep
To get a child yet by his own confession,
And yet his wife has seven.
YELLOWHAMMER
What, by Sir Walter?   250
ALLWIT
Sir Walter's like to keep 'em, and maintain 'em,
In excellent fashion, he dares do no less sir.
YELLOWHAMMER
Life has he children too?
ALLWIT
Children? Boys thus high,
In their Cato and Cordelius.   255
YELLOWHAMMER
What, you jest sir!
ALLWIT
Why, one can make a verse,
And is now at Eton College.

241 *venting conies* selling rabbits

---

255 *Cato and Cordelius.* Dionysius Cato's *Disticha de Moribus*, written in
3rd or 4th century, and Marthurin Cordier's *Colloquia scholastica* (1564)
were famous textbooks.
258 *Eton College,* founded by Henry VI in 1440.

YELLOWHAMMER
O this news has cut into my heart coz.

ALLWIT
It had eaten nearer if it had not been prevented.   260
One Allwit's wife.

YELLOWHAMMER
Allwit? Foot I have heard of him,
He had a girl kursened lately?

ALLWIT
Ay, that work did cost the knight above a hundred mark.

YELLOWHAMMER
I'll mark him for a knave and villain for't,   265
A thousand thanks and blessings, I have done with him.

ALLWIT
[Aside] Ha, ha, ha, this knight will stick by my ribs still,
I shall not lose him yet, no wife will come,
Where'er he woos, I find him still at home, ha, ha!   Exit

YELLOWHAMMER
Well grant all this, say now his deeds are black,   270
Pray what serves marriage, but to call him back;
I have kept a whore myself, and had a bastard,
By Mistress Anne, in Anno—
I care not who knows it; he's now a jolly fellow,
H'as been twice warden, so may his fruit be,   275
They were but base begot, and so was he;
The knight is rich, he shall be my son-in-law,
No matter so the whore he keeps be wholesome,
My daughter takes no hurt then, so let them wed,
I'll have him sweat well e'er they go to bed.   280

Enter MAUDLIN

MAUDLIN
O husband, husband.

YELLOWHAMMER
How now Maudlin?

MAUDLIN
We are all undone, she's gone, she's gone.

YELLOWHAMMER
Again? Death which way?

260 *prevented* anticipated
278 *wholesome* free of the pox
280 *sweat well* to cure possible infection

275 *warden.* See note to II, i, 71.

MAUDLIN
   Over the houses: 285
   Lay the waterside, she's gone forever else.
YELLOWHAMMER
   O venturous baggage!   *Exit* [*with* MAUDLIN]

       Enter TIM *and* TUTOR

TIM
   Thieves, thieves, my sister's stolen,
   Some thief hath got her:
   O how miraculously did my father's plate 'scape,   290
   'Twas all left out, tutor.
TUTOR
   Is't possible?
TIM
   Besides three chains of pearl and a box of coral.
   My sister's gone, let's look at Trig stairs for her;
   My mother's gone to lay the Common stairs   295
   At Puddle wharf, and at the dock below
   Stands my poor silly father. Run sweet tutor, run.
                        Exit [*with* TUTOR]

[Act IV, Scene ii]

Enter both the TOUCHWOODS

TOUCHWOOD SENIOR
   I had been taken brother by eight sergeants,
   But for the honest watermen; I am bound to them,
   They are the most requiteful'st people living,
   For as they get their means by gentlemen,
   They are still the forwardest to help gentlemen.   5
   You heard how one 'scaped out of the Blackfriars
   But a while since from two or three varlets
   Came into the house with all their rapiers drawn,
   As if they'd dance the sword dance on the stage,

286 *Lay* set watch on
1 *sergeants* sheriff's officers

---

294 *Trig stairs*. A landing place on the Thames at the bottom of Trig Lane.
295–296 *Common stairs at Puddle wharf*. About two hundred yards upstream from Trig stairs; the 'dock' is presumably Puddle Dock.
  6 *Blackfriars* theatre, the second known 'private' theatre; used by boys' companies 1600–1608 and by the King's Men 1608–1642.

With candles in their hands like chandlers' ghosts,   10
Whilst the poor gentleman so pursued and bandied
Was by an honest pair of oars safely landed.
TOUCHWOOD JUNIOR
  I love them with my heart for't.

Enter three or four WATERMEN

1 WATERMAN
  Your first man sir.
2 WATERMAN
  Shall I carry you gentlemen with a pair of oars?   15
TOUCHWOOD SENIOR
  These be the honest fellows;
  Take one pair, and leave the rest for her.
TOUCHWOOD JUNIOR
  Barn Elms.
TOUCHWOOD SENIOR
  No more brother.   [*Exit*]
1 WATERMAN
  Your first man.   20
2 WATERMAN
  Shall I carry your worship?
TOUCHWOOD JUNIOR
  Go, and you honest watermen that stay,
  Here's a French crown for you;
  There comes a maid with all speed to take water,
  Row her lustily to Barn Elms after me.   25
2 WATERMAN
  To Barn Elms, good sir: make ready the boat Sam,
  We'll wait below.   *Exit*
            Enter MOLL

11 *bandied* hit at
23 *French crown* French *écu*, worth about the same as the English
   crown (5s)

---

10 *candles.* Ghosts carried symbolic objects so that they could be recog-
   nized; the ruffians needed candles to find their victim in the roofed
   Blackfriars theatre.
13 s.d. WATERMEN. The taxicab men of the time; John Taylor, the 'water-
   poet', reckoned that by 1614 2,000 small boats plied the river about
   London and between Windsor and Gravesend 40,000 lives were maintained by their labour; Queenhithe was their headquarters and they
   were renowned for strong language.
18 *Barn Elms.* A resort of lovers and duellists opposite Hammersmith.

TOUCHWOOD JUNIOR
What made you stay so long?
MOLL
I found the way more dangerous than I looked for.
TOUCHWOOD JUNIOR
Away quick, there's a boat waits for you,   30
And I'll take water at Paul's wharf, and overtake you.
MOLL
Good sir do, we cannot be too safe.   [*Exeunt*]

    Enter SIR WALTER, YELLOWHAMMER, TIM *and* TUTOR

SIR WALTER
Life, call you this close keeping?
YELLOWHAMMER
She was kept under a double lock.
SIR WALTER
A double devil.   35
TIM
That's a buff sergeant, tutor, he'll ne'er wear out.
YELLOWHAMMER
How would you have women locked?
TIM
With padlocks father, the Venetian uses it,
My tutor reads it.
SIR WALTER
Heart, if she were so locked up, how got she out?   40
YELLOWHAMMER
There was a little hole looked into the gutter,
But who would have dreamt of that?
SIR WALTER
A wiser man would.
TIM
He says true, father, a wise man for love will seek every
hole: my tutor knows it.   45

36 *buff* tough, whitish leather from oxhide usually worn by sergeants
41 *looked* opened

---

31 *Paul's wharf* was between Puddle wharf and Queenhithe.
38 *Venetian* women were believed lascivious and weak and the men cruel
    and oppressive.
39 *reads.* Advises, or in the normal sense; cf. 'The sly Venetian locked his
    lady's ware,/Yet through her wit Actaeon's badge he bare' (*Ariosto's*
    Satires, [Tr.] G. Markham (1608), sig. K2^r).
45 *knows.* Ironic, as the tutor has probably cuckolded Yellowhammer.

TUTOR
  Verum poeta dicit.
TIM
  Dicit Virgilius, father.
YELLOWHAMMER
  Prithee talk of thy gills somewhere else, she's played the
  gill with me: where's your wise mother now?
TIM
  Run mad I think, I thought she would have drowned herself;   50
  she would not stay for oars, but took a smelt boat: sure I
  think she be gone afishing for her.
YELLOWHAMMER
  She'll catch a goodly dish of gudgeons now,
  Will serve us all to supper.

  Enter MAUDLIN *drawing* MOLL *by the hair, and* WATERMEN

MAUDLIN
  I'll tug thee home by the hair.   55
WATERMEN
  Good mistress spare her.
MAUDLIN
  Tend your own business.
WATERMEN
  You are a cruel mother.   *Ex[eunt]*
MOLL
  O my heart dies!
MAUDLIN
  I'll make thee an example for all the neighbours' daughters.   60
MOLL
  Farewell life.
MAUDLIN
  You that have tricks can counterfeit.
YELLOWHAMMER
  Hold, hold Maudlin.
MAUDLIN
  I have brought your jewel by the hair.
YELLOWHAMMER
  She's here knight.   65

  49 *gill* wench
  51 *smelt* any small and easily caught fish, therefore applied, like
     gudgeon, to a simpleton

  ────────────────────────────────────

  46–47 'The poet speaks truth' 'Virgil says it'.

SIR WALTER
  Forbear or I'll grow worse.

TIM
  Look on her, tutor, she hath brought her from the water
  like a mermaid; she's but half my sister now, as far as the
  flesh goes, the rest may be sold to fishwives.

MAUDLIN
  Dissembling cunning baggage.   70

YELLOWHAMMER
  Impudent strumpet.

SIR WALTER
  Either give over both, or I'll give over:
  Why have you used me thus unkind mistress?
  Wherein have I deserved?

YELLOWHAMMER
  You talk too fondly sir, we'll take another course and   75
  prevent all; we might have done't long since; we'll lose no
  time now, nor trust to't any longer: tomorrow morn as
  early as sunrise we'll have you joined.

MOLL
  O bring me death tonight, love pitying fates,
  Let me not see tomorrow up upon the world.   80

YELLOWHAMMER
  Are you content sir, till then she shall be watched?

MAUDLIN
  Baggage you shall.   *Exit [with* MOLL *and* YELLOWHAMMER]

TIM
  Why father, my tutor and I will both watch in armour.

TUTOR
  How shall we do for weapons?

TIM
  Take you no care for that, if need be I can send for conquer-   85
  ing metal tutor, ne'er lost day yet; 'tis but at Westminster
  —I am acquainted with him that keeps the monuments; I
  can borrow Harry the Fifth's sword, 'twill serve us both to
  watch with.   *Exit [with* TUTOR]

SIR WALTER
  I never was so near my wish, as this chance   90
  Makes me; ere tomorrow noon,
  I shall receive two thousand pound in gold,

---

  86 *Westminster*. The Abbey monuments could be viewed for a penny;
  since Henry V's armour had been stolen, with his head of silver, Tim's
  boast is probably an empty one.

And a sweet maidenhead
Worth forty.

Enter TOUCHWOOD JUNIOR *with a* WATERMAN

TOUCHWOOD JUNIOR
O thy news splits me.   95
WATERMAN
Half drowned, she cruelly tugged her by the hair,
Forced her disgracefully, not like a mother.
TOUCHWOOD JUNIOR
Enough, leave me like my joys.   *Exit* WATERMAN
Sir saw you not a wretched maid pass this way?
Heart villain, is it thou?   *Both draw and fight*   100
SIR WALTER
Yes slave, 'tis I.
TOUCHWOOD JUNIOR
I must break through thee then, there is no stop
That checks my tongue and all my hopeful fortunes,
That breast excepted, and I must have way.
SIR WALTER
Sir I believe 'twill hold your life in play.   105
TOUCHWOOD JUNIOR
Sir you'll gain the heart in my breast at first.
SIR WALTER
There is no dealing then, think on the dowry for two
thousand pounds.
TOUCHWOOD JUNIOR
O now 'tis quit sir.
SIR WALTER
And being of even hand, I'll play no longer.   110
TOUCHWOOD JUNIOR
No longer slave?
SIR WALTER
I have certain things to think on,
Before I dare go further.
TOUCHWOOD JUNIOR
But one bout?
I'll follow thee to death, but ha't out.   *Ex[eunt]*   115

94 *forty*. Later in the 17th century 150 gold *écus* (about £37) and a year's
   keep were quoted as the price of a virgin in Venice. (See F. Henriques,
   Prostitution and Society (1963) II, p. 89.)
105 *play*. Middleton later used gaming imagery with great effect in *Women
   Beware Women* II, ii, when the conversation during a chess game forms
   an ironic commentary on a seduction.

Act V, [Scene i]

Enter ALLWIT, *his* WIFE, *and* DAVY DAHUMMA

MISTRESS ALLWIT
A misery of a house.
ALLWIT
What shall become of us?
DAVY
I think his wound be mortal.
ALLWIT
Think'st thou so Davy?
Then am I mortal too, but a dead man Davy;   5
This is no world for me, when e'er he goes,
I must e'en truss up all, and after him Davy,
A sheet with two knots, and away.

Enter SIR WALTER *led in hurt* [*by two* SERVANTS]

DAVY   O see sir,
How faint he goes, two of my fellows lead him.
MISTRESS ALLWIT
O me!   10
ALLWIT
Hyday, my wife's laid down too, here's like to be
A good house kept, when we are altogether down;
Take pains with her good Davy, cheer her up there,
Let me come to his worship, let me come. [*Exeunt* SERVANTS]
SIR WALTER
Touch me not villain, my wound aches at thee,   15
Thou poison to my heart.
ALLWIT   He raves already,
His senses are quite gone, he knows me not;
Look up an't like your worship, heave those eyes,
Call me to mind, is your remembrance lost?
Look in my face, who am I an't like your worship?   20
SIR WALTER
If any thing be worse than slave or villain,
Thou art the man.
ALLWIT   Alas his poor worship's weakness,
He will begin to know me by little and little.
SIR WALTER
No devil can be like thee.
ALLWIT   Ah poor gentleman,

8 *sheet* a shroud, with knots at the head and feet

Methinks the pain that thou endurest. 25

SIR WALTER

Thou know'st me to be wicked, for thy baseness
Kept the eyes open still on all my sins,
None knew the dear account my soul stood charged with
So well as thou, yet like Hell's flattering angel
Would'st never tell me on't, let'st me go on, 30
And join with death in sleep, that if I had not waked
Now by chance, even by a stranger's pity,
I had everlastingly slept out all hope
Of grace and mercy.

ALLWIT Now he is worse and worse,
Wife, to him wife, thou wast wont to do good on him. 35

MISTRESS ALLWIT

How is't with you sir?

SIR WALTER Not as with you,
Thou loathsome strumpet: some good pitying man
Remove my sins out of my sight a little;
I tremble to behold her, she keeps back
All comfort while she stays; is this a time, 40
Unconscionable woman, to see thee?
Art thou so cruel to the peace of man,
Not to give liberty now? The devil himself
Shows a far fairer reverence and respect
To goodness than thyself; he dares not do this, 45
But parts in time of penitence, hides his face;
When man withdraws from him, he leaves the place;
Hast thou less manners, and more impudence,
Than thy instructor? Prithee show thy modesty,
If the least grain be left, and get thee from me. 50
Thou should'st be rather locked many rooms hence,
From the poor miserable sight of me,
If either love or grace had part in thee.

MISTRESS ALLWIT

He is lost for ever.

ALLWIT Run sweet Davy quickly, [*Exit* DAVY]
And fetch the children hither—sight of them 55
Will make him cheerful straight.

SIR WALTER O death! Is this
A place for you to weep? What tears are those?
Get you away with them, I shall fare the worse

25 *Methinks* I understand
35 *do good* with a pun on 'do' = 'copulate'
46 *parts* (part Q) departs

As long as they are aweeping; they work against me;
There's nothing but thy appetite in that sorrow,   60
Thou weep'st for lust, I feel it in the slackness
Of comforts coming towards me;
I was well till thou began'st to undo me;
This shows like the fruitless sorrow of a careless mother
That brings her son with dalliance to the gallows,   65
And then stands by, and weeps to see him suffer.

Enter DAVY *with the* CHILDREN

DAVY
There are the children sir, an't like your worship,
Your last fine girl, in troth she smiles,
Look, look, in faith sir.
SIR WALTER   O my vengeance,
Let me for ever hide my cursed face   70
From sight of those, that darkens all my hopes,
And stands between me and the sight of Heaven;
Who sees me now, he too and those so near me,
May rightly say, I am o'er-grown with sin;
O how my offences wrestle with my repentance,   75
It hath scarce breath—
Still my adulterous guilt hovers aloft,
And with her black wings beats down all my prayers
Ere they be half way up; what's he knows now
How long I have to live? O what comes then?   80
My taste grows bitter, the round world, all gall now,
Her pleasing pleasures now hath poisoned me,
Which I exchanged my soul for;
Make way a hundred sighs at once for me.
ALLWIT
Speak to him Nick.
NICK   I dare not, I am afraid.   85
ALLWIT
Tell him he hurts his wounds Wat, with making moan.
SIR WALTER
Wretched, death of seven.

65 *dalliance* over indulgence
73 *he* (ho Q) Dyce emends 'O too', Bullen gives 'O, O', saying
'Probably my reading is not correct, but I dislike Dyce's "O
too"', and Wall leaves the Q reading, commenting, 'Apparently
it is an exclamation, and is at least as expressive as it stands as
either Dyce or Bullen have made it'. If 'he' is accepted, it can be
taken to refer to 'who'
87 *seven* Mrs Allwit's children by Sir Walter

ALLWIT
  Come let's be talking somewhat to keep him alive.
  Ah sirrah Wat, and did my lord bestow that jewel on thee,
  For an epistle thou mad'st in Latin?   90
  Thou art a good forward boy, there's great joy on thee.
SIR WALTER
  O sorrow!
ALLWIT   Heart will nothing comfort him?
  If he be so far gone, 'tis time to moan;
  Here's pen, and ink, and paper, and all things ready,
  Will't please your worship for to make your will?   95
SIR WALTER
  My will? Yes, yes, what else? Who writes apace now?
ALLWIT
  That can your man Davy an't like your worship,
  A fair, fast, legible hand.
SIR WALTER
  Set it down then:
  Imprimis, I bequeath to yonder wittol,   100
  Three times his weight in curses—
ALLWIT
  How?
SIR WALTER
  All plagues of body and of mind—
ALLWIT
  Write them not down Davy.
DAVY
  It is his will, I must.   105
SIR WALTER
  Together also,
  With such a sickness, ten days ere his death.
ALLWIT
  There's a sweet legacy,
  I am almost choked with't.
SIR WALTER
  Next I bequeath to that foul whore his wife,   110
  All barrenness of joy, a drouth of virtue,
  And dearth of all repentance: for her end,
  The common misery of an English strumpet,
  In French and Dutch, beholding ere she dies

114 *French*. A reference to syphilis, 'the French disease'.
114 *Dutch*. A general epithet of inferiority; a 'Dutch widow' was a harlot.
    (See Middleton's *A Trick to Catch the Old One* III, iii, 15–17.)

Confusion of her brats before her eyes,   115
And never shed a tear for it.

Enter a SERVANT

SERVANT   Where's the knight?
O sir, the gentleman you wounded is newly departed.
SIR WALTER
Dead? Lift, lift, who helps me?
ALLWIT
Let the law lift you now, that must have all,
I have done lifting on you, and my wife too.   120
SERVANT
You were best lock yourself close.
ALLWIT   Not in my house sir,
I'll harbour no such persons as men-slayers,
Lock yourself where you will.
SIR WALTER   What's this?
MISTRESS ALLWIT   Why husband!
ALLWIT
I know what I do wife.
MISTRESS ALLWIT   You cannot tell yet;
For having killed the man in his defence,   125
Neither his life, nor estate will be touched husband.
ALLWIT
Away wife, hear a fool, his lands will hang him.
SIR WALTER
Am I denied a chamber?
What say you forsooth?
MISTRESS ALLWIT
Alas sir, I am one that would have all well,   130
But must obey my husband. Prithee love
Let the poor gentleman stay, being so sore wounded,
There's a close chamber at one end of the garret
We never use, let him have that I prithee.
ALLWIT
We never use? You forget sickness then,   135
And physic times: is't not a place for easement?

120 *lifting* stealing, but also used with a sexual sense with reference to
    Mrs Allwit
127 *hear a fool* listen to the silly woman!
133 *close chamber* small room, here a privy

127 *lands.* His lands will be forfeited to the Crown, since he's a murderer, so
    he is more likely to hang.

Enter a SERVANT

SIR WALTER
  O death! Do I hear this with part
  Of former life in me? What's the news now?
SERVANT
  Troth worse and worse, you're like to lose your land
  If the law save your life sir, or the surgeon.   140
ALLWIT
  Hark you there wife.
SIR WALTER
  Why how sir?
SERVANT
  Sir Oliver Kix's wife is new quickened;
  That child undoes you sir.
SIR WALTER   All ill at once.
ALLWIT
  I wonder what he makes here with his consorts?   145
  Cannot our house be private to ourselves,
  But we must have such guests? I pray depart sirs,
  And take your murderer along with you—
  Good he were apprehended ere he go,
  He's killed some honest gentleman; send for officers.   150
SIR WALTER
  I'll soon save you that labour.
ALLWIT   I must tell you sir,
  You have been somewhat bolder in my house
  Than I could well like of; I suffered you
  Till it stuck here at my heart; I tell you truly
  I thought you had been familiar with my wife once.   155
MISTRESS ALLWIT
  With me? I'll see him hanged first; I defy him,
  And all such gentlemen in the like extremity.
SIR WALTER
  If ever eyes were open, these are they;
  Gamesters farewell, I have nothing left to play.
                              Exit [with SERVANTS]
ALLWIT
  And therefore get you gone sir.
DAVY   Of all wittols,   160
  Be thou the head. Thou the grand whore of spitals.   *Exit*

145 *consorts* companions

---

150 *officers* of the watch could arrest offenders and take them before the
  constable or justice of the peace.

ALLWIT
  So, since he's like now to be rid of all,
  I am right glad I am so well rid of him.
MISTRESS ALLWIT
  I knew he durst not stay, when you named officers.
ALLWIT
  That stopped his spirits straight;   165
  What shall we do now wife?
MISTRESS ALLWIT
  As we were wont to do.
ALLWIT
  We are richly furnished wife, with household stuff.
MISTRESS ALLWIT
  Let's let out lodgings then,
  And take a house in the Strand.
ALLWIT   In troth a match wench: 170
  We are simply stocked with cloth of tissue cushions,
  To furnish out bay windows: push, what not that's quaint
  And costly, from the top to the bottom.
  Life, for furniture, we may lodge a countess:
  There's a close-stool of tawny velvet too,   175
  Now I think on't wife.
MISTRESS ALLWIT   There's that should be sir;
  Your nose must be in every thing.
ALLWIT   I have done wench;
  And let this stand in every gallant's chamber:
  There's no gamester like a politic sinner,
  For who e'er games, the box is sure a winner.   180
               Exit [*with* MISTRESS ALLWIT]

---

175 *close-stool* a chamber pot in a stool or box
176 *There's that* . . . There's everything there ought to be

---

170 *Strand*, the most fashionable part of London, running from Temple Bar
    to Charing Cross.
172 *bay windows* were used by whores to display themselves (cf. Middleton,
    Hengist, King of Kent III, i, 143); Allwit's use of 'quaint' indicates an
    intention of setting up a brothel.
180 *box*. The box into which money was placed by gamesters as a kind of
    cover charge; 'every player, at the first hand he draweth, payeth a
    crown to the box, by way of relief towards the house charges'. (G.
    Walker, *A Manifest Detection of the Most Vile and Detestable Use of
    Diceplay*, ed. J. O. Halliwell (1850), p. 12.) Allwit is comparing himself
    to the box, which no matter what happens, contains the money. There
    may also be a pun on 'box' = 'coffin'.

[Act V, Scene ii]

Enter YELLOWHAMMER *and his* WIFE

MAUDLIN
O husband, husband, she will die, she will die,
There is no sign but death.
YELLOWHAMMER   'Twill be our shame then.
MAUDLIN
O how she's changed in compass of an hour.
YELLOWHAMMER
Ah my poor girl! Good faith thou wert too cruel
To drag her by the hair.   5
MAUDLIN
You would have done as much sir,
To curb her of her humour.
YELLOWHAMMER
'Tis curbed sweetly, she catched her bane o'th' water.

Enter TIM

MAUDLIN
How now Tim?
TIM
Faith busy, mother, about an epitaph   10
Upon my sister's death.
MAUDLIN
Death! She is not dead I hope?
TIM
No: but she means to be, and that's as good,
And when a thing's done, 'tis done,
You taught me that, mother.   15
YELLOWHAMMER
What is your tutor doing?
TIM
Making one too, in principal pure Latin,
Culled out of Ovid de Tristibus.
YELLOWHAMMER
How does your sister look, is she not changed?

17 *principal* excellent
18 *Ovid de Tristibus* a commonly used Latin text book

---

14 *And . . . done.* Dyce suggests an allusion to a game called 'A thing
done', citing Jonson's *Cynthia's Revels* IV, 3, 160–170; the context there
is bawdy.

TIM

    Changed? Gold into white money was never so changed,   20
    As is my sister's colour into paleness.

           Enter MOLL [*led by* SERVANTS]

YELLOWHAMMER

    O here she's brought, see how she looks like death.

TIM

    Looks she like death, and ne'er a word made yet?
    I must go beat my brains against a bed post,
    And get before my tutor.   [*Exit*]

YELLOWHAMMER   Speak, how dost thou?   25

MOLL

    I hope I shall be well, for I am as sick at heart
    As I can be.

YELLOWHAMMER 'Las my poor girl,

    The doctor's making a most sovereign drink for thee,
    The worst ingredient, dissolved pearl and amber;
    We spare no cost girl.

MOLL   Your love comes too late,   30

    Yet timely thanks reward it. What is comfort,
    When the poor patient's heart is past relief?
    It is no doctor's art can cure my grief.

YELLOWHAMMER

    All is cast away then;
    Prithee look upon me cheerfully.   35

MAUDLIN

    Sing but a strain or two, thou wilt not think
    How 'twill revive thy spirits: strive with thy fit,
    Prithee sweet Moll.

MOLL

    You shall have my good will, mother.

MAUDLIN

    Why well said wench.   40

---

  25 *get* beget [a poem]

  29 *pearl and amber* were believed to have great medicinal properties;
     Robert Boyle says that the 'reducing of pearls to a fine powder affords a
     rich medicine' (*Works* (1772) p. 133), and a solution of amber with spirit
     of wine is 'a friend to the stomach, the entrails, the nervous parts, and
     even the head' (*Ibid.*, p. 329).
  37 *strive . . . fit.* (i) struggle with your condition, which betokens death;
     (ii) put up a fight by singing a strain.

[MOLL *sings*]   THE SONG

> Weep eyes, break heart,
> My love and I must part;
> Cruel fates true love do soonest sever,
> O, I shall see thee, never, never, never.
> O happy is the maid whose life takes end,   45
> Ere it knows parent's frown, or loss of friend.
> Weep eyes, break heart,
> My love and I must part.

Enter TOUCHWOOD SENIOR *with a letter*

MAUDLIN
  O, I could die with music: well sung girl.
MOLL
  If you call it so, it was.   50
YELLOWHAMMER
  She plays the swan, and sings herself to death.
TOUCHWOOD SENIOR
  By your leave sir.
YELLOWHAMMER
  What are you sir? Or what's your business pray?
TOUCHWOOD SENIOR
  I may be now admitted, though the brother
  Of him your hate pursued, it spreads no further;   55
  Your malice sets in death, does it not sir?
YELLOWHAMMER
  In death?
TOUCHWOOD SENIOR He's dead: 'twas a dear love to him,
  It cost him but his life, that was all sir:
  He paid enough, poor gentleman, for his love.
YELLOWHAMMER
  There's all our ill removed, if she were well now.   60
  Impute not sir, his end to any hate
  That sprung from us; he had a fair wound brought that.
TOUCHWOOD SENIOR
  That helped him forward, I must needs confess:
  But the restraint of love, and your unkindness,
  Those were the wounds that from his heart drew blood;   65
  But being past help, let words forget it too:

56 *sets* declines, wanes

---

51 *swan.* Swans were believed to sing only before they died; cf. the madrigal,
  'The Silver Swan', by Orlando Gibbons.

Scarcely three minutes ere his eyelids closed
And took eternal leave of this world's light,
He wrote this letter, which by oath he bound me,
To give to her own hands; that's all my business.   70

YELLOWHAMMER
You may perform it then, there she sits.

TOUCHWOOD SENIOR
O with a following look.

YELLOWHAMMER
I trust me sir, I think she'll follow him quickly.

TOUCHWOOD SENIOR
Here's some gold
He willed me to distribute faithfully amongst your servants.   75

YELLOWHAMMER
'Las what doth he mean sir?

TOUCHWOOD SENIOR
How cheer you mistress?

MOLL
I must learn of you sir.

TOUCHWOOD SENIOR
Here's a letter from a friend of yours,
And where that fails, in satisfaction   80
I have a sad tongue ready to supply.

MOLL
How does he, ere I look on't?

TOUCHWOOD SENIOR
Seldom better, h'as a contented health now.

MOLL
I am most glad on't.

MAUDLIN
Dead sir?   85

YELLOWHAMMER
He is. Now wife let's but get the girl
Upon her legs again, and to church roundly with her.

MOLL
O sick to death he tells me:
How does he after this?

TOUCHWOOD SENIOR
Faith feels no pain at all, he's dead sweet mistress.   90

MOLL
Peace close mine eyes.

72 *following* as though she were about to follow Touchwood Junior
   in death

YELLOWHAMMER

  The girl, look to the girl wife.

MAUDLIN

  Moll, daughter, sweet girl speak,
  Look but once up, thou shalt have all the wishes of thy
    heart   95
  That wealth can purchase.

YELLOWHAMMER

  O she's gone for ever, that letter broke her heart.

TOUCHWOOD SENIOR

  As good now, then, as let her lie in torment,
  And then break it.

                    Enter SUSAN

MAUDLIN

  O Susan, she thou lovedst so dear is gone.   100

SUSAN

  O sweet maid!

TOUCHWOOD SENIOR

  This is she that helped her still,
  I've a reward here for thee.

YELLOWHAMMER

  Take her in,
  Remove her from our sight, our shame, and sorrow.   105

TOUCHWOOD SENIOR

  Stay, let me help thee, 'tis the last cold kindness
  I can perform for my sweet brother's sake.

  [*Exeunt* TOUCHWOOD SENIOR, SUSAN *and* SERVANTS, *carrying* MOLL]

YELLOWHAMMER

  All the whole street will hate us, and the world
  Point me out cruel: it is our best course wife,
  After we have given order for the funeral,   110
  To absent ourselves, till she be laid in ground.

MAUDLIN

  Where shall we spend that time?

YELLOWHAMMER

  I'll tell thee where wench, go to some private church,
  And marry Tim to the rich Brecknock gentlewoman.

MAUDLIN

  Mass a match,   115
  We'll not lose all at once, somewhat we'll catch.

                    Exit [*with* YELLOWHAMMER]

113 *private* secret

---

97 *heart*. See note to I, ii, 55–56.

[Act V, Scene iii]

Enter SIR OLIVER *and* SERVANTS

SIR OLIVER

Ho, my wife's quickened, I am a man for ever,
I think I have bestirred my stumps i'faith:
Run, get your fellows all together instantly,
Then to the parish church, and ring the bells.

1 SERVANT

It shall be done sir.   [*Exit*]   5

SIR OLIVER

Upon my love I charge you villain, that you make a bonfire
before the door at night.

2 SERVANT

A bonfire sir?

SIR OLIVER

A thwacking one I charge you.

2 SERVANT

[*Aside*] This is monstrous.   [*Exit*]   10

SIR OLIVER

Run, tell a hundred pound out for the gentleman
That gave my wife the drink, the first thing you do.

3 SERVANT

A hundred pounds sir?

SIR OLIVER

A bargain, as our joys grows,
We must remember still from whence it flows,   15
Or else we prove ungrateful multipliers:
The child is coming, and the land comes after;
The news of this will make a poor Sir Walter.
I have struck it home i'faith.

3 SERVANT

That you have marry sir.   20
But will not your worship go to the funeral
Of both these lovers?

SIR OLIVER

Both, go both together?

3 SERVANT

Ay sir, the gentleman's brother will have it so,

---

19 *struck it home* given a winning blow; a *double entendre*

4, 6 *bells*. Churchbells were rung and *bonfires* lit to announce important
happenings.

'Twill be the pitifullest sight; there's such running,   25
Such rumours, and such throngs, a pair of lovers
Had never more spectators, more men's pities,
Or women's wet eyes.

SIR OLIVER
My wife helps the number then?

3 SERVANT
There's such a drawing out of handkerchers,   30
And those that have no handkerchers, lift up aprons.

SIR OLIVER
Her parents may have joyful hearts at this,
I would not have my cruelty so talked on,
To any child of mine, for a monopoly.

3 SERVANT
I believe you sir.   35
'Tis cast so too, that both their coffins meet,
Which will be lamentable.

SIR OLIVER
Come, we'll see't.   *Ex[eunt]*

[Act V, Scene iv]

*Recorders dolefully playing. Enter at one door the coffin of the
gentleman, solemnly decked, his sword upon it, attended by many
in black, his brother being the chief mourner. At the other door, the
coffin of the virgin, with a garland of flowers, with epitaphs pinned
on it, attended by maids and women. Then set them down one right
over against the other, while all the company seem to weep and
mourn; there is a sad song in the music room. [The company includes* SIR OLIVER *and* LADY KIX, MR *and* MRS ALLWIT, SUSAN *and
a* PARSON]

TOUCHWOOD SENIOR
Never could death boast of a richer prize
From the first parent, let the world bring forth
A pair of truer hearts; to speak but truth
Of this departed gentleman, in a brother,
Might by hard censure be called flattery,   5

s.d. *Recorders* were the most common wind instruments of the time, and
frequently mentioned in plays (e.g. *Hamlet* III, ii, 367–96). The stage
direction here corroborates the evidence of the de Witt sketch that the
Swan had two doors; the music room mentioned here is not shown in
the drawing, however. The pantomime is discussed in D. Mehl, *The
Elizabethan Dumb Show* (1965), pp. 148–9.

Which makes me rather silent in his right
Than so to be delivered to the thoughts
Of any envious hearer starved in virtue,
And therefore pining to hear others thrive.
But for this maid, whom envy cannot hurt   10
With all her poisons, having left to ages
The true, chaste monument of her living name,
Which no time can deface, I say of her
The full truth freely, without fear of censure;
What nature could there shine, that might redeem   15
Perfection home to woman, but in her
Was fully glorious; beauty set in goodness
Speaks what she was; that jewel so infixed,
There was no want of any thing of life
To make these virtuous precedents man and wife.   20

ALLWIT
Great pity of their deaths.

ALL
Ne'er more pity.

LADY KIX
It makes a hundred weeping eyes, sweet gossip.

TOUCHWOOD SENIOR
I cannot think, there's any one amongst you,
In this full fair assembly, maid, man, or wife,   25
Whose heart would not have sprung with joy and gladness
To have seen their marriage day?

ALL
It would have made a thousand joyful hearts.

TOUCHWOOD SENIOR
Up then apace, and take your fortunes,
Make these joyful hearts, here's none but friends.   30
    [MOLL *and* TOUCHWOOD JUNIOR *rise from their coffins*]

ALL
Alive sir? O sweet dear couple.

TOUCHWOOD SENIOR
Nay, do not hinder 'em now, stand from about 'em,
If she be caught again, and have this time,
I'll ne'er plot further for 'em, nor this honest chambermaid
That helped all at a push.

TOUCHWOOD JUNIOR   Good sir apace.   35

10 *But* only
20 *precedents* examples worthy to be followed
35 *at a push* energetically
35 s.p. TOUCHWOOD JUNIOR ed. (TOUCHWOOD SENIOR Q)

PARSON

Hands join now, but hearts for ever,
Which no parent's mood shall sever.
You shall forsake all widows, wives, and maids:
You, lords, knights, gentlemen, and men of trades:
And if in haste, any article misses,   40
Go interline it with a brace of kisses.

TOUCHWOOD SENIOR

Here's a thing trolled nimbly. Give you joy brother,
Were't not better thou should'st have her,
Than the maid should die?

MISTRESS ALLWIT

To you sweet mistress bride.   45

ALL

Joy, joy to you both.

TOUCHWOOD SENIOR

Here be your wedding sheets you brought along with you,
you may both go to bed when you please to.

TOUCHWOOD JUNIOR

My joy wants utterance.

TOUCHWOOD SENIOR

Utter all at night then brother.   50

MOLL

I am silent with delight.

TOUCHWOOD SENIOR

Sister, delight will silence any woman,
But you'll find your tongue again, among maidservants,
Now you keep house, sister.

ALL

Never was hour so filled with joy and wonder.   55

TOUCHWOOD SENIOR

To tell you the full story of this chambermaid,
And of her kindness in this business to us,
'Twould ask an hour's discourse. In brief 'twas she
That wrought it to this purpose cunningly.

ALL

We shall all love her for't.   60

Enter YELLOWHAMMER *and his* WIFE

40 *article* part of the ceremony; legal term, as is *interline*
41 *brace* pair, and also a clasp or support
47 *wedding sheets* the shrouds
50 *Utter* with a similar meaning to 'sing' at II, i, 52

ALLWIT
  See who comes here now.
TOUCHWOOD SENIOR
  A storm, a storm, but we are sheltered for it.
YELLOWHAMMER
  I will prevent you all, and mock you thus,
  You, and your expectations; I stand happy,
  Both in your lives, and your hearts' combination.   65
TOUCHWOOD SENIOR
  Here's a strange day again.
YELLOWHAMMER   The knight's proved villain,
  All's come out now, his niece an arrant baggage;
  My poor boy Tim is cast away this morning,
  Even before breakfast: married a whore
  Next to his heart.
ALL   A whore?
YELLOWHAMMER   His niece forsooth.   70
ALLWIT
  I think we rid our hands in good time of him.
MISTRESS ALLWIT
  I knew he was past the best, when I gave him over.
  What is become of him pray sir?
YELLOWHAMMER
  Who, the knight? He lies i'th' knight's ward now.
  Your belly, lady, begins to blossom, there's no peace for him,   75
  His creditors are so greedy.
SIR OLIVER
  Mr Touchwood, hear'st thou this news?
  I am so endeared to thee for my wife's fruitfulness,
  That I charge you both, your wife and thee,
  To live no more asunder for the world's frowns;   80
  I have purse, and bed, and board for you:
  Be not afraid to go to your business roundly,
  Get children, and I'll keep them.
TOUCHWOOD SENIOR   Say you so sir?
SIR OLIVER
  Prove me, with three at a birth, and thou dar'st now.
TOUCHWOOD SENIOR
  Take heed how you dare a man, while you live sir,   85

70 *Next to his heart* (a) closest in love (b) on an empty stomach
74 *knight's ward.* There were four grades of accommodation in the two
    Counters (debtors' prisons), and the Fleet Prison: the master's side, the
    knight's ward, the twopenny ward and the hole, for those who could pay
    nothing; cf. Chapman, Jonson and Marston, *Eastward Ho!* V, ii, 42–44.

That has good skill at his weapon.

Enter TIM *and* WELSH GENTLEWOMAN

SIR OLIVER

Foot, I dare you sir.

YELLOWHAMMER

Look gentlemen, if ever you saw the picture
Of the unfortunate marriage, yonder 'tis.

WELSH GENTLEWOMAN

Nay good sweet Tim.   90

TIM

Come from the university,
To marry a whore in London, with my tutor too?
O tempora! O mors!

TUTOR

Prithee Tim be patient.

TIM

I bought a jade at Cambridge,   95
I'll let her out to execution tutor,
For eighteen pence a day, or Brainford horse races;
She'll serve to carry seven miles out of town well.
Where be these mountains? I was promised mountains,
But there's such a mist, I can see none of 'em.   100
What are become of those two thousand runts?
Let's have about with them in the meantime.
A vengeance runt thee.

MAUDLIN   Good sweet Tim have patience.

TIM

Flectere si nequeo superos Acheronta movebo, mother.

MAUDLIN

I think you have married her in logic Tim.   105
You told me once, by logic you would prove
A whore an honest woman, prove her so Tim
And take her for thy labour.

TIM   Troth I thank you.
I grant you I may prove another man's wife so,

---

88 *saw* ed. (say Q)   95 *jade* horse   96 *execution* movement in riding
103 *runt* reprove, admonish (though the meaning is stronger here)

---

 93 'O time! O death!' Tim probably meant to say *mores*, 'manners'.
 97 *Brainford*, Brentford (see note II, ii, 215); horseracing was one of the
    entertainments for visitors; Tim's speech is *double entendre*.
104 'Since I cannot prevail upon the powers above, I shall work on the
    lower regions' (Virgil, *Aeneid*, VII, 312).

But not mine own.

MAUDLIN   There's no remedy now Tim,   110
You must prove her so as well as you may.

TIM
Why then my tutor and I will about her,
As well as we can.
Uxor non est meretrix, ergo falacis.

WELSH GENTLEWOMAN
Sir if your logic cannot prove me honest,   115
There's a thing called marriage, and that makes me honest.

MAUDLIN
O there's a trick beyond your logic Tim.

TIM
I perceive then a woman may be honest according to the
English print, when she is a whore in the Latin. So much
for marriage and logic. I'll love her for her wit, I'll pick out   120
my runts there: and for my mountains, I'll mount upon—

YELLOWHAMMER
So fortune seldom deals two marriages
With one hand, and both lucky: the best is,
One feast will serve them both: marry, for room
I'll have the dinner kept in Goldsmiths' Hall,   125
To which kind gallants, I invite you all.   [*Exeunt*]

FINIS

121 *upon* . . . the lacuna is in Q

---

114 'A wife is not a whore, therefore you are wrong'.
125 *Goldsmiths' Hall.* The hall of the Goldsmiths' Company, in Foster Lane
    off Cheapside, 'a proper house, but not large' (*Survey*, I, 305).

APPENDIX A

THOMAS CAMPION uses the following epigram in the sixth chapter of his *Observations in the Art of English Poesie* (1602) as an illustration of English trochaic verse. (See Introduction, p. xiv.) The text here is modernized from that in *Campion's Works*, ed. Percival Vivian (Oxford, 1909), p. 46.

The Eighth Epigram

Barnzy stiffly vows that he's no cuckold,
Yet the vulgar everywhere salutes him
With strange signs of horns, from every corner;
Wheresoe'er he comes, a sundry 'Cuckoo'
Still frequents his ears; yet he's no cuckold.   5
But this Barnzy knows that his Matilda,
Scorning him, with Harvy plays the wanton.
Knows it? Nay desires it, and by prayers
Daily begs of heav'n that it for ever
May stand firm for him; yet he's no cuckold.   10
And 'tis true, for Harvy keeps Matilda,
Fosters Barnzy, and relieves his household,
Buys the cradle, and begets the children,
Pays the nurses, every charge defraying,
And thus truly plays Matilda's husband: 15
So that Barnzy now becomes a cipher,
And himself th'adulterer of Matilda.
Mock not him with horns, the case is altered;
Harvy bears the wrong, he proves the cuckold.

A similar theme, but with added religious and commercial implications, is found in a Jacobean ballad in the Harleian MS. (3910, fols. 41ᵛ–42). The text here is modernized from the version in *Old English Ballads 1553–1625*, ed. Hyder E. Rollins (Cambridge, 1920), pp. 196–197.

1

Who would not be a cuckold,
To have a handsome wife?
Who would not be a wittol,
To lead a merry life?
    Though many do disdain it,   5
    And scorn to have the name,

Yet others entertain it,
And never blush for shame.

2

The good-wife, like a peacock,
She jets in brave attire;   10
The good-man, like a meacock,[1]
Sits smoking o'er the fire:
  He never dares reprove her,
  But lets her have her will;
  Nor cares how many loves her,   15
  So she the purse do fill.

3

Some men attain to maces,
Through bounty of their dames,
And cover all disgraces,
If well they play their games;   20
  But when the sole commanding
  Amongst the females fall,
  For want of understanding
  They commonly mar all.

4

Nor doth alone the city   25
Such precedents afford:
In court, the more the pity,
Some ladies play the lord:
  And then to be in fashion,
  She turns Catholical—   30
  O vile abomination,
  The Pope can pardon all!

5

Are women thus devoted
To levities by kind?
Or are the men so doted   35
To see and yet be blind?
  But profit and promotion
  The world do over-rule
  And counterfeit devotion
  Can make the wise a fool.   40

[1] *meacock* an effeminate and cowardly man.

APPENDIX B

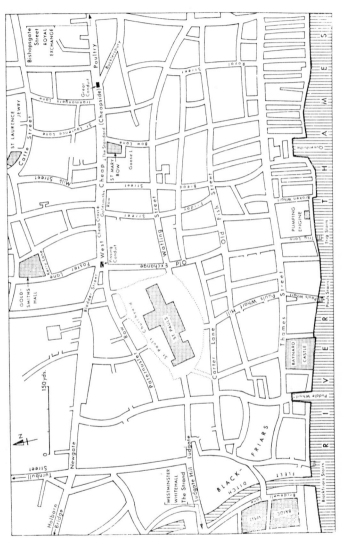

Map showing parts of Elizabethan London mentioned in A Chaste Maid in Cheapside.